FOOLPROOF

· TRAYBAKES ·

FOOLPROOF

• TRAYBAKES •

60 SIMPLE AND DELICIOUS
ONE-TIN BAKES

KATIE MARSHALL

PHOTOGRAPHY BY
RITA PLATTS

Quadrille

Quadrille, Penguin Random House UK,
One Embassy Gardens, 8 Viaduct Gardens,
London SW11 7BW

Quadrille Publishing Limited is part of
the Penguin Random House group of
companies whose addresses can be found
at global.penguinrandomhouse.com

Penguin
Random House
UK

Published by Quadrille in 2025

www.penguin.co.uk

A CIP catalogue record for this book is
available from the British Library

ISBN 9781837833238
10 9 8 7 6 5 4 3 2 1

Colour reproduction by F1

Printed in China by C&C Offset Printing Co., Ltd.

The authorised representative in the EEA is
Penguin Random House Ireland, Morrison
Chambers, 32 Nassau Street, Dublin D02
YH68.

Penguin Random House is committed to
a sustainable future for our business, our
readers and our planet. This book is made
from Forest Stewardship Council® certified
paper.

Managing Director
Sarah Lavelle

Assistant Editor
Sofie Shearman

Series Designer
Emily Lapworth

Designer
Katy Everett

Photographer
Rita Platts

Food Stylist
Katie Marshall

Food Stylist Assistants
Jessica Geddes, Lucy Cottle
and Mimi Phillips

Prop Stylist
Max Robinson

Head of Production
Stephen Lang

Production Manager
Sabeena Atchia

CONTENTS

INTRODUCTION

The traybake is the go-to bake for the party-going, public transport-taking, long distance-travelling crowd feeder. Its beauty lies in its versatility, transportability and, of course, its volume. Every rectangular creation can be sliced into 16–24 pieces (fewer for particularly sweet-toothed grazers, or more if you have an impromptu increase in guests). Traybakes are adaptable and sturdy and tend to keep well (there are fewer exposed edges to go stale) – and are also incredibly nostalgic. For me, they're a reminder of my mum making big carrot cakes for road trips (see my recipe on page 66): a snack for the road, then a treat supply for the holiday. The recipe was imported from my auntie in America, so it seemed extra special.

As well as meeting all the criteria for an afternoon treat, a traybake can seamlessly segue into catering for a celebration. Its rectangular shape means that, left in its tin, it's easily wrapped or covered and can fit neatly into the bottom of a wide-based, flat-bottomed bag. Chuck on some candles and a bit of extra décor (edible glitter and food-safe flowers, if you're me) and – hey presto – birthday/christening/any occasion covered! Leftovers can then be handily smuggled home in the same way, too. I use a lidded baking tray for ease of transportation. It's also helpful for keeping your cake fresher for longer!

A note on tins

One of the joys of a traybake is its sheer size: you need only bake once to feed many hungry mouths. There's no faffing with layering, crumb-coating and complex decoration. Traybakes can be no-frills, humble bakes, just bringing the magic of being a delicious concoction.

I use a 20 x 30 x 5cm (8 x 12 x 2in) non-stick tin as I've found it's perfect as a brownie pan/giant carrot cake tin/ the thing you'd use to make a strange, 90s-style birthday sponge. The dimensions are ideal for baking in bulk.

Getting started with baking

In this book, I've tried to keep the instructions simple – methods are easy to follow, without too many steps, and you don't need any fancy equipment. You might even notice some repetition with some of the methods, because once I've realized that something works for me, I like to stick to it. Most of the recipes can be prepped and in the oven within ten minutes. Maximum flavour and minimal effort is a failsafe mantra of mine.

Useful items

- All the bakes are perfectly achievable with a balloon whisk, a wooden spoon and sheer muscle, but if you have electric beaters or a stand mixer, they will make the job easier.

- It's useful to have a variety of prep and mixing bowls. Having a suitable vessel for each task makes following the recipe smoother, and lets you weigh out your ingredients in advance.

- An oven thermometer is a great investment. Oven temperatures really do vary, and thermostats all read a bit differently, so if you have a thermometer (one that you can read from outside the oven is even better), you can find and maintain the optimum temperature to avoid any carcinogenic malfunctions or dreadfully soggy bottoms.

- Digital scales are a must – baking is a science and the recipes in this book all have been rigorously tested to make sure the weights, quantities and timings work. For best results, measure accurately and use the right ingredients!

Tips, tricks and techniques

Always thoroughly line your tins as per the recipe instructions. In general, a thin layer of room temperature butter topped with a large sheet of baking parchment that's eased into the tin then folded or trimmed in the corners, will stop your cakes sticking to the tin.

It's good practice to have all your ingredients weighed out and lined up before you start mixing. This avoids a panic when you realize you're low on an ingredient mid-bake, but also means you'll get the most out of the recipe: your beaten eggs won't be going flat nor your baking agent deflating while you fumble in the back of a cupboard. (That's another reason why it's good to have a few different bowls.) A stitch in time definitely saves nine.

To melt chocolate, you can place it in a heatproof bowl over a pan of barely simmering water, or blast it in short bursts in the microwave. Going gently means you will prevent it from catching or burning. White chocolate is sensitive, so keep a close eye on it.

A note on ingredients

Almost all the ingredients I've used are widely available (the bougie cherries in the Black Forest Cake on page 15 might be a little harder to find) and you may find you have many of them knocking about already.

Some recipes call for vanilla bean paste and others for vanilla extract. Vanilla bean paste is more concentrated, giving a more authentic taste of Madagascan vanilla, and as a result it's quite expensive (but a worthwhile investment, in my opinion!). Vanilla extract, on the other hand, gives more of a 'sense' of the flavour (think old-school vanilla ice cream). Feel free to use vanilla extract in place of the bean paste; it will make only a subtle change to the end bake.

All eggs are medium and should be room temperature before you begin.

Temperature
It's important to follow instructions for the temperature of the ingredients. If a recipe calls for softened butter, don't try to whisk fridge-cold stuff instead. Similarly, don't try to skip or reduce the chilling time if the recipe requires it. Remember: baking is a science!

DOs and DON'Ts

DON'T skip preheating your oven. If the oven isn't at temperature when a chemical raising agent goes in, you'll end up with a flat cake.

DO line your tins with non-stick baking parchment, or as per the instructions in the recipe.

DO have everything lined up and ready to go!

DO follow the instructions for chilling and refrigerating – it will make the recipe more foolproof *and* more delicious.

DON'T judge doneness on timings alone as ovens vary. Test your sponges are cooked by inserting a skewer or toothpick into the centre – when it's cooked, the skewer will come out clean.

FRUITY SPONGES

There's so much variety to be had when it comes to fruit, from tinned peaches to jarred pears, to the banana going brown and spotty in your fruit bowl. That burst of natural sweetness is joy in the making. Here you'll find something to fit every occasion, from afternoon tea to dessert, and each recipe has its own seasonal nod.

BANOFFEE CAKE

Banoffee pie is an English invention. Who would have known?! Here, I've slightly revamped the amazingly decadent combination of toffee and banana, hiding delicious chunks of fudge in a moist banana sponge. Topped with pillowy whipped cream, this cake has a shorter shelf-life than some of the other sponges – it will last around 3 days in the fridge, if there's any left! If homemade caramel is intimidating, substitute for shop-bought – just melt it slightly first.

300g (10½fl oz) sunflower oil, plus extra
  for greasing
3 ripe bananas (about 360g/12½oz with
  skins on), peeled and mashed
3 eggs, beaten
2 tsp vanilla bean paste
405g (14¼oz) soft light brown sugar
405g (14¼oz) plain (all-purpose) flour
1½ tsp baking powder
1½ tsp bicarbonate of soda
  (baking soda)
1 tsp salt
125g (4½oz) fudge, chopped into rough
  1cm (½in) pieces

For the toppings
120g (4¼oz) salted butter
120g (4¼oz) soft light brown sugar
480ml (16¼fl oz) double (heavy) cream
1 tsp flaky sea salt
1–2 bananas, sliced
grated chocolate, to decorate (optional)

Preheat the oven to 160°C fan/180°C/350°F/Gas mark 4. Grease and line the base and sides of a 20 × 30cm (8 × 12in) baking tray.

Put the mashed bananas, sunflower oil, eggs and vanilla bean paste into a jug and mix to combine.

Tip the brown sugar into a large bowl and use your fingers to get rid of any lumps (you might even want to sift it). Sift in the flour, baking powder, bicarbonate of soda and salt, then toss through the fudge pieces. Add the banana mixture and use a balloon whisk to combine.

Spoon or pour the mixture into the prepared baking tray and bake for 45 minutes, or until a skewer inserted comes out clean. Leave to cool to room temperature.

Meanwhile, prepare the toppings. To make the caramel, combine the butter and brown sugar in a small saucepan over a low–medium heat and stir gently with a wooden spoon until they have melted together. Increase the heat (do not stir) and bring to the boil, then remove from the heat and carefully add 80ml (2½fl oz) of the cream – it might splutter. Add the flaky sea salt and whisk to combine. Transfer to a bowl and allow to cool to a spreadable consistency. You can put it in the fridge to speed things along, if needed.

When the cake is cool and the caramel is spreadable, whisk the remaining 400ml (14fl oz) cream to soft peaks. Spread half the caramel over the sponge, then top with the whipped cream. Drizzle with the remaining caramel, then arrange the banana slices over the top and scatter with the grated chocolate, if using.

Serves 18
–
Prep 20 mins
–
Bake 45 mins

LEMON DRIZZLE CAKE

My aim with this drizzle cake was to create a lip-smacking citrus kick, and I think I managed it with six lemons! Poking holes all over the surface of the cake is an essential step: the lemony sugar soaks through and the drizzle permeates every last piece.

225g (8oz) salted butter, at room temperature, plus extra for greasing
300g (10½oz) caster (superfine) sugar
zest of 4 lemons (reserve the juice for the drizzle below)
6 eggs, beaten
275g (9¾oz) self-raising flour
80ml (5 tbsp) double (heavy) cream
pinch of flaky sea salt

For the drizzle
zest of 1 lemon, juice of 6 (about 200ml/7fl oz juice)
270g (9½oz) caster (superfine) sugar

Preheat the oven to 160°C fan/180°C/350°F/Gas mark 4. Grease and line the base and sides of a 20 × 30cm (8 × 12in) baking tray.

Put the sugar into a large mixing bowl, or the bowl of a stand mixer, and add the lemon zest. Mix to combine, then add the butter and beat until light and creamy. Slowly add the eggs and mix until combined. Sift in half the flour, then fold it through, along with the cream and flaky sea salt. Sift in the remaining flour and fold it through until incorporated.

Transfer to the prepared baking tray and smooth the surface. Bake on a middle shelf for 30–35 minutes, or until a skewer inserted comes out clean, then remove from the oven.

Leave to cool in the tin for 20 minutes, then pierce lots of holes in the surface of the cake with a skewer, going straight down to the bottom (don't be shy about doing about 180 pricks!).

Combine the drizzle ingredients in a bowl, then pour over the surface of the cake, allowing the drizzle to seep through the holes and into the sponge.

Allow to cool completely before slicing into 24 squares and serving.

Serves 24
–
Prep 15 mins
–
Bake 35 mins

BLACK FOREST CAKE

Cherries and chocolate make an undeniably sophisticated combination. I've used Amarena cherries, which are grown in Modena and Bologna and preserved in syrup. They're worth the investment (not least for their gorgeous jar), but if you can't find them, use tinned cherries instead. In place of the ready-made syrup from the jar, just simmer down the liquid from the tinned cherries with a couple of tablespoons of sugar, then leave to cool, to create your own drizzling syrup.

110g (3¾oz) salted butter, plus extra for greasing
110g (3¾oz) dark chocolate, broken into pieces
3 tbsp cocoa powder
280ml (9½fl oz) boiling water
140ml (4¾fl oz) buttermilk
290g (10¼oz) plain (all-purpose) flour
2½ tsp bicarbonate of soda (baking soda)
1 tsp salt
340g (12oz) light soft brown sugar
3 eggs, beaten
2 tsp vanilla bean paste
200g (7oz) Amarena cherries (drained weight), plus 8–10 tbsp syrup from the jar, for drizzling

For the buttercream
350g (12oz) icing (confectioners') sugar
175g (6oz) salted butter, at room temperature
45ml (3 tablespoons) double (heavy) cream
12–15 Amarena cherries and their syrup

Preheat the oven to 160°C fan/180°C/350°F/Gas mark 4. Grease and line a 20 × 30cm (8 × 12in) baking tray.

Combine the butter and chocolate in a small saucepan over a low heat and gently heat until melted (if you prefer, you can do this in short bursts in the microwave, stirring between each one). Set aside to cool slightly.

Sift the cocoa powder into a bowl and add just enough boiling water to form a smooth paste, stirring continuously. Then add the rest of the water and mix to combine. Stir in the buttermilk. Set aside to cool slightly.

Sift the flour, bicarbonate of soda and salt into a large bowl and add the brown sugar. Beat the eggs and vanilla bean paste into the cocoa and water mixture, then slowly add half of this mixture to the bowl of dry ingredients, whisking as you go, to make a smooth batter. Next, add the chocolate and butter mix, then add the remaining cocoa and water mixture. Mix it all together to fully combine.

Pour the batter into the prepared baking tray and evenly scatter the cherries over the top. Bake for 40 minutes, or until a skewer inserted comes out clean. Leave to cool completely.

When cool, carefully flip the cake upside-down on to a board, then drizzle over 8–10 tablespoons of syrup from the cherry jar.

To make the buttercream, sift the icing sugar into a large mixing bowl, or the bowl of a stand mixer, then add the butter and cream. Whisk until light and fluffy, then spread over the sponge. Dot with the cherries and their syrup and serve.

Serves 18
–
Prep 15 mins
–
Bake 40 mins

Fruity Sponges

CHERRY AND ALMOND CAKE

This cake takes its cue from one of my favourite flavour combinations – that of the Bakewell tart. The marzipan melts into sticky pools of intense almondy flavour, in a delicious almond-infused sponge. The buried glacé cherries are my favourite – I've been known to eat them straight from the pot.

250g (9oz) unsalted butter, at room temperature, plus extra for greasing
250g (9oz) caster (superfine) sugar
5 eggs, beaten
175g (6oz) self-raising flour
½ tsp baking powder
150g (5½oz) ground almonds
200g (7oz) marzipan
1 tsp almond extract
200g (7oz) glacé cherries, halved

For the topping
60g (2oz) icing (confectioners') sugar
juice of ½ lemon
10g (½oz) toasted flaked almonds, to decorate

Preheat the oven to 160°C fan/180°C/350°F/Gas mark 4. Grease and line the base and sides of a 20 × 30cm (8 × 12in) baking tray.

Put the butter and caster sugar into a large mixing bowl, or the bowl of a stand mixer, and beat until light and fluffy. Slowly add the eggs and mix until combined, sifting in 1–2 tablespoons of the flour if it starts to split. Sift in the flour and baking powder, then add the ground almonds and fold to incorporate. Make pinches of the marzipan and add these to the mixture, along with the almond extract, then fold everything together.

Spoon half of the batter into the base of the baking tin, then scatter half the cherries on top. Spoon over the remaining cake batter, followed by the rest of the cherries, pushing them down into the mixture with the back of a metal spoon. Bake for 40–45 minutes, or until a skewer inserted comes out clean. Cool in the tin.

To make the icing, sift the icing sugar into a bowl, then add the lemon juice and stir to combine until the mixture has a loose consistency – you want it to be a little thicker than cream. Drizzle this over the cooled cake, then scatter with the almonds before slicing and serving.

Serves 18
–
Prep 15 mins
–
Bake 45 mins

COCONUT AND LIME CAKE

Inspired by the amazing tropical flavours of south Asia, this recipe uses powdered coconut as a substitute for some of the flour. By using a high-speed blender to blitz the coconut, you end up with a fine, flour-like texture. If you don't have a blender, standard desiccated coconut would work fine – you might just have a slightly coarser crumb.

150g (5½oz) coconut oil (at room temperature, but not melted), plus extra for greasing
300g (10½oz) caster (superfine) sugar
5 egg whites
220g (8oz) coconut milk
100g (3½oz) soured cream
280g (10oz) self-raising flour
1 tsp fine salt
100g (3½oz) desiccated (dried shredded) coconut, ground to a powder in a high-speed blender
zest of 5 limes (save the juice for the topping below)

For the topping
25g (1oz) desiccated (dried shredded) coconut
200g (7oz) icing (confectioners') sugar
35–40ml (2–3 tablespoons) lime juice
zest of 1 lime

Preheat the oven to 160°C fan/180°C/350°F/Gas mark 4. Grease and line the base and sides of a 20 × 30cm (8 × 12in) baking tray.

Put the coconut oil and caster sugar into a large mixing bowl, or the bowl of a stand mixer. Whisk until combined (it might take about 5 minutes to come together). Gradually add the egg whites, mixing until incorporated. Add the coconut milk and soured cream and whisk again briefly until combined and glossy. Now sift in the flour and salt, then add the ground coconut and lime zest and mix until just combined. Spoon into the prepared baking tray.

Bake for 35–40 minutes, or until a skewer inserted comes out clean. Allow to cool completely in the tin.

Meanwhile, to prepare the topping, spread out the desiccated coconut on a baking tray and bake at 160°C fan/180°C/350°F/ Gas mark 4 for 4–5 minutes until golden. Set aside to cool.

Sift the icing sugar into a bowl, then add the lime juice a little at a time until you have a thick but spreadable, honey-like consistency. Spread the icing over the cooled cake and scatter with the toasted coconut and lime zest before slicing and serving.

Serves 18
–
Prep 15 mins
–
Bake 45 mins

PEACH MELBA CAKE

This cake is as beautiful as it is delicious. Fresh, juicy peaches (or nectarines) and plump, seasonal raspberries come together to create a sponge that tastes exactly like summer.

300g (10½oz) salted butter, at room temperature, plus extra for greasing
300g (10½oz) golden caster (superfine) sugar
6 eggs, beaten
250g (9oz) self-raising flour
75g (2½oz) ground almonds
3 peaches, 2 stoned and chopped into 1cm (½in) dice, 1 stoned and sliced
200g (7oz) raspberries

For the glaze
3 tbsp peach or apricot conserve

Preheat the oven to 160°C fan/180°C/350°F/Gas mark 4. Grease and line the base and sides of a 20 × 30cm (8 × 12in) baking tray.

Put the butter and sugar into a large mixing bowl, or the bowl of a stand mixer, and whisk until light and fluffy. Slowly add the eggs, sifting in 2 tablespoons of the flour if the mixture starts to split. Once combined, sift in the flour and add the ground almonds, then fold through until incorporated. Carefully fold in the chopped peaches.

Spoon half the batter into the prepared baking tray, then scatter half the raspberries on top, pushing them down gently into the mixture. Top with the remaining cake batter, followed by the rest of the raspberries, again pushing them gently into the mixture. Arrange the peach slices on top, pushing them gently into the mixture.

Bake for 45–50 minutes, or until a skewer inserted comes out clean. Leave to cool to room temperature.

For the glaze, put the peach or apricot conserve in a small saucepan over a low heat and add 2 teaspoons of water, stirring until combined (if you prefer, you can do this in a bowl in the microwave). You can pass the glaze through a sieve (strainer) to get rid of any chunks, if you like. Brush the glaze all over the cake. Allow to cool completely before serving.

Serves 18
–
Prep 15 mins
–
Bake 50 mins

ORANGE AND ALMOND CAKE

Inspired by a traditional cake hailing from Morocco, this bake has a magical combination of sweetness and slight bitterness, thanks to the inclusion of the whole orange – rind and all. The recipe will work a thousand times more easily if you have access to a food processor, but can alternatively be achieved with some dedicated fine chopping. Plus, it's naturally gluten free.

3 unwaxed oranges
butter or oil, for greasing
5 eggs, beaten
75g (2½oz) soft light brown sugar
175g (6oz) golden caster
    (superfine) sugar
200g (7oz) ground almonds
150g (5½oz) gluten-free self-raising flour
1 tsp gluten-free baking powder

For the topping
150g (5½oz) caster (superfine) sugar
zest of 1 orange and juice of ½ (about
    50ml/3 tablespoons)
20g (¾oz) toasted flaked almonds

Put the oranges in a saucepan and pour over enough boiling water to cover. Place over a high heat and bring to the boil. Place a lid that is slightly too small for the pan over the oranges, so that they stay submerged. Boil for 1 hour–1 hour 10 minutes, then drain and allow to cool. (Alternatively, pierce the oranges with a sharp knife, then place in a microwave-proof bowl and pour over enough boiling water to cover. Cover the bowl with cling film/plastic wrap. Pierce some holes in the cling film, then microwave for 10–15 minutes, or until a sharp knife can easily pierce the oranges. Drain and leave to cool.)

When you're ready to make the cake, preheat the oven to 160°C fan/180°C/350°F/Gas mark 4. Grease and line the base and sides of a 20 × 30cm (8 × 12in) baking tray.

Cut the cooled oranges in half and remove any pips (seeds), then transfer to a food processor and blitz to a pulp.

In a large bowl, mix together the eggs, both sugars and ground almonds, then sift in the flour and baking powder. Add the orange pulp and mix it all together with a balloon whisk. Spoon the batter into the prepared baking tray and bake for 40 minutes, or until a skewer inserted comes out clean. Allow to cool to room temperature.

To make the topping, combine the caster sugar with the orange zest and juice in a saucepan over a medium heat. Bring to a rapid simmer and bubble until the mixture starts to thicken, but not to the point of becoming a syrup. Pour this over the cake and spread it out evenly, then scatter with the flaked almonds. Allow to cool completely before serving.

Serves 18
–
Prep 85 mins
–
Bake 40 mins

PLUM CRUMBLE CAKE

Perfectly fitting the criteria for some autumnal comfort, this sponge is great straight-up, but can readily be swamped in hot custard or doused in cream for a warming family dessert.

For the crumble topping

100g (3½oz) cold salted butter, cubed, plus extra for greasing
150g (5½oz) plain (all-purpose) flour
50g (2oz) rolled oats
75g (2½oz) golden caster (superfine) sugar
45g (1¾oz) demerara sugar
pinch of salt

For the sponge

200g (7oz) salted butter, at room temperature
200g (7oz) golden caster (superfine) sugar
4 eggs, beaten
1 tsp ground cinnamon
200g (7oz) self-raising flour
300g (10½oz) ripe but firm plums, stoned and sliced into 5mm (¼in) slices

whipped cream or custard, to serve (optional)

Preheat the oven to 160°C fan/180°C/350°F/Gas mark 4. Grease and line the base and sides of a 20 × 30cm (8 × 12in) baking tray.

Start by preparing the crumble topping. Rub the butter and flour together with your fingertips in a large bowl until the mixture resembles sand. Add the oats, both sugars and salt, then mix together, pinching some of the mixture to make clumps. Refrigerate until needed.

To make the sponge, put the butter and sugar into the into a large mixing bowl, or the bowl of a stand mixer. Whisk continuously until light and fluffy. Slowly add the eggs, continuing to whisk or with the motor still running. Once incorporated, sift in the cinnamon and flour and fold through until combined.

Spoon the sponge batter into the prepared baking tray, then arrange the plum slices on top. Sprinkle the crumble mixture evenly over the top and bake for 35–40 minutes, or until a skewer inserted comes out clean.

Allow to cool to room temperature, then slice and serve with whipped cream or warming custard, if you like.

Serves 18
–
Prep 15 mins
–
Bake 40 mins

APPLE CAKE

This cosy cake makes excellent use of an abundance of autumn apples. I've used Bramley because they get super soft and leave no bite, but try swapping them for Braeburn or Jazz, or whatever is left in the fruit bowl.

200g (7oz) salted butter, at room
    temperature, plus extra for greasing
360g (12½oz) self-raising flour
1 tbsp ground cinnamon
½ tsp ground ginger
200g (7oz) soft light brown sugar
3 eggs, beaten
100ml (3½fl oz) whole milk
250–300g (10½oz) Bramley apples,
    peeled, cored and diced
50g (2oz) demerara sugar

For the topping (optional)
120g (4¼oz) icing (confectioners') sugar
1 tsp ground cinnamon

custard or cream, to serve

Preheat the oven to 160°C fan/180°C/350°F/Gas mark 4. Grease and line the base and sides of a 20 × 30cm (8 × 12in) baking tray.

Put the butter, flour, cinnamon, ginger and soft light brown sugar into a large mixing bowl, or the bowl of a stand mixer, and whisk continuously or with the whisk attachment until the butter has been incorporated. In a small jug, mix together the eggs and milk, then incorporate this into the mixture, whisking until it just comes together. Gently fold through the apple pieces.

Spoon the mixture into the prepared baking tray and sprinkle with the demerara sugar.

Bake for 35 minutes, or until a skewer inserted comes out clean. Leave to cool for 10 minutes.

If making the topping, sift the icing sugar into a bowl, then add the cinnamon. Add 20–25ml (4 teaspoons–1½ tablespoons) of water, a little at a time, until you have a thick but pourable consistency. Drizzle over the whole cake.

Serve and eat warm, with custard, or allow to cool fully and serve with cream.

Serves 18
–
Prep 15 mins
–
Bake 35 mins

PINEAPPLE UPSIDE-DOWN CAKE

Full. Retro. Vibes! This sponge was my gateway into cake-baking – the most simple batter, piled on top of syrup, pineapple and (of course) glacé cherries. I love this cake warm, particularly when you get an edge where the syrup has started to caramelize and tastes more like toffee.

300g (10½oz) unsalted butter, at room temperature, plus extra for greasing
2 × 432g (15¼oz) cans pineapple rings, drained
230g (8oz) golden syrup
100g (3½oz) glacé cherries (about 12)
300g (10½oz) golden caster (superfine) sugar
6 eggs, beaten
300g (10½oz) self-raising flour
1 tsp baking powder
1 tsp fine salt
3 tbsp whole milk
1 tsp vanilla bean paste

cream, to serve (optional)

Preheat the oven to 170°C fan/190°C/375°F/Gas mark 5. Grease and line the base and sides of a 20 × 30cm (8 × 12in) baking tray.

Arrange the pineapple rings on a plate lined with paper towels and leave them to dry a little.

Pour the golden syrup into the base of the prepared baking tray, then put it into the oven for 2 minutes so it is starting to melt and spreads out evenly.

Remove from the oven and arrange as many of the pineapple rings as possible in the base of the baking tray (you should be able to fit 4 along and 3 down). Break up a couple of the leftover rings to fill any gaps; you might end up with a couple spare. Place a cherry in the middle of each complete pineapple ring. Set aside.

Put the butter and sugar into a large mixing bowl, or the bowl of a stand mixer, and whisk together until light and fluffy. Slowly add the eggs, whisking continuously or with the motor still running. Once incorporated, sift in the flour, baking powder and salt and fold in, then add the milk and vanilla bean paste and mix to combine.

Spoon the batter over the top of the pineapples in the tray and bake for 45–50 minutes, or until a skewer inserted comes out clean.

Allow to cool in the tin for 10 minutes before turning out on to a wire rack. Delicious eaten warm or cold, with a drizzle of cream, if you like.

Serves 18
–
Prep 15 mins
–
Bake 52 mins

TROPICAL FRUIT CAKE

I love fruit cake so much that I don't think it should be confined to Christmas, or even winter. I've given this a tropical twist which legitimises its presence all year round. The raisins benefit from an overnight soak in rum, for a grown-up taste of the Caribbean. Delicious with a cup of tea, of course.

500g (1lb 2oz) mixed dried fruit
100g (3½oz) dried mango,
　roughly chopped
100g (3½oz) dried pineapple,
　roughly chopped
100ml (3½fl oz) dark spiced rum
200g (7oz) canned pineapple, drained
　weight, finely chopped, plus 75ml
　(5 tbsp) of the juice
225g (8oz) salted butter, at room
　temperature, plus extra for greasing
230g (8oz) soft light brown sugar
4 eggs, beaten
150g (5oz) plain (all-purpose) flour
100g (3½oz) ground almonds
2 tsp ground cinnamon
½ tsp ground ginger

For the topping
icing (confectioners') sugar, for dusting
450g (1lb) golden marzipan
2 tbsp apricot jam

Combine all the dried fruits and rum in a saucepan. Add the juice from the canned pineapple and bring to a simmer. Stir, then take off the heat and cover with a lid. Leave for a few hours, or overnight.

When you're ready to bake, preheat the oven to 160°C fan/180°C/350°F/Gas mark 4. Grease and line the base and sides of a 20 × 30cm (8 × 12in) baking tray.

Put the butter and sugar into a large mixing bowl, or the bowl of a stand mixer, and whisk together until light and creamy. Slowly add the eggs, mixing to incorporate, then sift in the flour. Add the almonds and spices, followed by the canned pineapple, and fold to combine. Add the dried fruit and rum mixture and fold it all together, then spoon into the prepared baking tray.

Bake for 40–45 minutes, or until a skewer inserted comes out clean. Allow to cool completely.

Lightly dust the work surface with icing sugar. Roll out the marzipan until it's about the same size as the cake. Brush the top of the cake with the apricot jam, then lay the marzipan on top. Cut into squares and serve.

Serves 18–24
—
**Prep 15 mins,
plus soaking**
—
Bake 45 mins

STRAWBERRY AND WHITE CHOCOLATE CAKE

This gorgeous summery cake tastes absolutely amazing with sweet, ripe, in-season strawberries. The melted white chocolate gives a slight fudginess, a bit like a blondie. You're welcome.

250g (9oz) salted butter, at room temperature, plus extra for greasing
200g (7oz) white chocolate, broken into pieces
200g (7oz) caster (superfine) sugar
3 eggs, plus 2 egg whites
150g (5oz) soured cream
2 tsp vanilla bean paste
250g (9oz) self-raising flour
400g (14oz) strawberries, hulled and diced into rough 1cm (½in) chunks

For the topping
200g (7oz) white chocolate, broken into pieces
140g (5oz) cream cheese
70g (2¼oz) salted butter, at room temperature
300g (10½oz) icing (confectioners') sugar
5 strawberries, sliced

Preheat the oven to 160°C fan/180°C/350°F/Gas mark 4. Grease and line a 20 × 30cm (8 × 12in) baking tray.

Melt the chocolate in short bursts in a heatproof bowl set over a pan of barely simmering water (if you prefer, you can do this in short bursts in the microwave, stirring between each one). Once melted, set aside to cool slightly.

Put the butter and sugar into a large mixing bowl, or the bowl of a stand mixer. Whisk until fluffy and pale, then add the 2 egg whites and continue to whisk for a few more minutes, until fully incorporated.

In a separate bowl or jug, combine the 3 remaining eggs with the soured cream and vanilla bean paste. Add this mixture to the mixture in the bowl or stand mixer, scraping down the sides of the bowl, and whisk to combine. Don't worry if it curdles slightly. Whisking continuously, pour in the melted chocolate. Once incorporated, sift in the flour and fold it through, then carefully fold through the strawberries.

Transfer the batter into the prepared baking tray and bake for 40–45 minutes, or until a skewer inserted comes out clean. Leave to cool completely.

Meanwhile, prepare the topping. Melt the chocolate in the same way as before, then set aside to cool slightly. Combine the cream cheese and butter in a bowl, or the bowl of a stand mixer, then sift in the icing sugar and whisk until smooth. Slowly pour in the chocolate and give it a final whisk.

Spread the frosting over the surface of the cooled cake and scatter over the sliced strawberries to decorate.

Serves 18
–
Prep 15 mins
–
Bake 45 mins

Fruity Sponges

LEMON AND BLUEBERRY TRAYBAKE

This is a deservedly classic flavour pairing which combines sweet and tart. The method of combining wet and dry ingredients makes the prep super simple, and means it's a great one for getting kids involved in. The batter isn't too sweet, so I've given it a thin icing – by re-baking the cake once warm, the icing starts to infuse into the surface, making it almost like a doughnut glaze.

80g (3oz) sunflower oil, plus extra
    for greasing
4 eggs
170g (6oz) natural yoghurt
50ml (3 tablespoons) milk
300g (10½oz) caster (superfine) sugar
340g (12oz) plain (all-purpose) flour
1 tbsp baking powder
zest of 4 lemons
300g (10½oz) blueberries

For the glaze
150g (5oz) icing (confectioners') sugar
juice of 1 lemon

Preheat the oven to 160°C fan/180°C/350°F/Gas mark 4. Grease and line the base and sides of a 20 × 30cm (8 × 12in) baking tray.

Combine the eggs, oil, yoghurt and milk in a jug. In a large mixing bowl, mix together the sugar, flour, baking powder, lemon zest and blueberries. Whisk in the liquid ingredients and mix until smooth.

Pour the batter into the prepared baking tray and bake for 35–40 minutes, or until a skewer inserted comes out clean. Remove from the oven and allow to cool in the tin for 20 minutes.

To prepare the glaze, sift the icing sugar into a bowl, then add the lemon juice and stir to combine. Pour the glaze evenly over the cake, then return it to the oven for 3 minutes for the glaze to set.

> Serves 18
> –
> Prep 5 mins
> –
> Bake 43 mins

Fruity Sponges

APPLE AND BLACKBERRY STREUSEL CAKE

A bake that just smacks of autumn. You could make this a wholesome, hand-picked bake by foraging your own blackberries or, if you have access to an apple tree, by using an autumnal windfall. I've used a melting method for the streusel topping to ensure a decadent, buttery texture, so the streusel almost melts into the cake topping. This doubles up as an excellent pudding.

For the streusel topping
100g (3½oz) salted butter, plus extra for greasing
150g (5oz) plain (all-purpose) flour
125g (4oz) soft light brown sugar
1 tsp ground cinnamon

For the sponge
200g (7oz) salted butter, at room temperature
200g (7oz) golden caster (superfine) sugar
4 eggs, beaten
1 tsp vanilla bean paste
175g (6oz) self-raising flour
50g (2oz) ground almonds
300g (10½oz) blackberries
400g (14oz) Bramley apples (about 2 medium apples) peeled, cored and diced into 1cm (½in) cubes
pinch of flaky sea salt
2 tsp icing (confectioners') sugar, for dusting

Preheat the oven to 160°C fan/180°C/350°F/Gas mark 4. Grease and line the base and sides of a 20 × 30cm (8 × 12in) baking tray.

Start by preparing the streusel topping. Melt the butter in a small saucepan over a low heat. Combine the flour, sugar and cinnamon in a bowl. Stir through the melted butter, forming clumps of mixture. Refrigerate until needed.

To make the sponge, put the butter and sugar into a large mixing bowl, or the bowl of a stand mixer, and whisk together until light and fluffy. Slowly add the eggs and vanilla, whisking continuously. Sift in the flour, then add the ground almonds and fold through until combined. Spoon into the prepared baking tray, then scatter the blackberries and apple chunks evenly over the top. Sprinkle over the streusel mixture, along with a generous pinch of flaky salt.

Bake for 40 minutes, or until a skewer inserted comes out clean. Allow to cool to room temperature, then dust with icing sugar before slicing and serving.

Serves 18
–
Prep 15 mins
–
Bake 40 mins

PINEAPPLE, ORANGE AND PASSION FRUIT CAKE

The wonderfully soft sponge ticks all the tropical boxes. The moist crumb is, in part, thanks to the vegetable oil – which also happens to be cheaper than butter. The seeds in the glaze give a wonderful crunch.

250g (9oz) sunflower oil, plus extra
    for greasing
300g (10½oz) plain (all-purpose) flour
300g (10½oz) caster (superfine) sugar
1 tsp bicarbonate of soda (baking soda)
1 tsp baking powder
½ tsp salt
3 eggs, beaten
425g (15oz) can pineapple, drained and
    chopped
zest of 2 oranges
pulp of 4 passion fruits

For the glaze
250g (9oz) icing (confectioners') sugar
pulp of 4 passion fruits
2–3 tablespoons orange juice

Preheat the oven to 160°C fan/180°C/350°F/Gas mark 4. Grease and line the base and sides of a 20 × 30cm (8 × 12in) baking tray.

Combine the flour, sugar, bicarbonate of soda, baking powder and salt in a large bowl. Mix the eggs, sunflower oil, pineapple pieces, orange zest and passion fruit pulp in a separate bowl or jug. Beat this into the dry mixture until combined. Pour or spoon the mixture into the prepared tray.

Bake for 45 minutes, or until a skewer inserted comes out clean. Allow to cool completely in the tin.

To make the glaze, sift the icing sugar into a bowl, then add the passion fruit pulp. Add the orange juice a little at a time until the consistency is thick but drizzleable. Drizzle the glaze over the cake, then return to the oven for 4 minutes. Allow the icing to harden before serving.

Serves 18–24
—
Prep 15 mins
—
Bake 49 mins

RHUBARB AND GINGER CAKE

Using three different types of ginger, this bake has layers of warmth, all of which complement the tartness of the rhubarb. I used regular rhubarb, but in the winter months, why not use the more tender pink (forced) rhubarb for wonderful pops of pink?

250g (9oz) salted butter, at room temperature, plus extra for greasing
250g (9oz) soft light brown sugar
5 eggs, beaten
250g (9oz) self-raising flour
1 tsp ground ginger
400g (14oz) rhubarb, trimmed and cut into rough 1cm (½in) chunks
6 stem ginger balls in syrup, finely chopped, plus 5 tbsp of the syrup
40g (1½oz) crystallised ginger, roughly chopped

cream, to serve (optional)

Preheat the oven to 160°C fan/180°C/350°F/Gas mark 4. Grease and line the base and sides of a 20 × 30cm (8 × 12in) baking tray.

Put the butter and sugar into a large mixing bowl, or the bowl of a stand mixer, and whisk together until light and fluffy. Slowly add the eggs, scraping down the sides of the bowl to make sure all the ingredients are incorporated. Sift in the flour, then add the ground ginger, rhubarb and chopped stem ginger, along with 2 tablespoons of the syrup, and fold through. Spoon into the prepared baking tray.

Bake for 40–50 minutes, or until a skewer inserted comes out clean. Leave to cool, then brush with the remaining 3 tablespoons of ginger syrup. Scatter with the crystallised ginger before slicing and serving with cream, if you like.

Serves 18
–
Prep 10 mins
–
Bake 50 mins

FRUIT COCKTAIL CAKE

Using tinned fruit is a great hack for having cake ingredients ever-ready in your larder. Using a lower quantity of butter compared to the other sponges, lots of its moisture comes from the fruit. I love the simplicity of this cake, with its humble soft brown sugar topping.

150g (5oz) salted butter, plus extra
    for greasing
250g (9oz) caster (superfine) sugar
3 eggs, beaten
250g (9oz) self-raising flour
2 × 415g (14½oz) cans fruit cocktail
    in juice, drained, plus 4 tbsp
    of the juice
75g (2½oz) light soft brown sugar

Preheat the oven to 160°C fan/180°C/350°F/Gas mark 4. Grease and line the base and sides of a 20 × 30cm (8 × 12in) baking tray.

Put the butter and sugar into a large mixing bowl, or the bowl of a stand mixer, and whisk together until well combined and turning light in colour. Slowly add the eggs, then whisk to combine. Sift in the flour, then briefly whisk it in, along with the fruit cocktail juice. Fold through the fruit cocktail fruit. Transfer into the prepared baking tray.

Scatter the brown sugar over the top and bake for 30 minutes, or until a skewer inserted comes out clean. Leave to cool completely in the tin before serving.

Serves 18
–
Prep 5 mins
–
Bake 30 mins

COMFORTING
SPONGES

When I say 'comfort', I mean sugar, and spice and all things nice. The Guinness Cake on page 64 will definitely beckon chimes of 'oooh' and 'mmm', while the Vanilla Sprinkle Cake on page 47 and the Coconut and Jam Sponge on page 61 are full of nostalgia! The Date Cake on page 50 is like an ambient, tamer version of sticky toffee pudding – is there any better contentment than that?

VANILLA SPRINKLE CAKE

This cake gives you license to go wild and raid the sprinkle drawer (or is just me who has one of those?). A simple vanilla sponge with a nice, thick coating of icing, this bake will transport you back to school dinners, complete with a nice soaking of custard.

250g (9oz) salted butter, at room temperature, plus extra for greasing
250g (9oz) caster (superfine) sugar
5 eggs, beaten
60ml (4 tbsp) whole milk
2½ tsp vanilla extract
250g (9oz) self-raising flour
1 tsp fine salt

For the topping
280g (10oz) icing (confectioners') sugar
50g (2oz) sprinkles

custard, to serve (optional)

Preheat the oven to 160°C fan/180°C/350°F/Gas mark 4. Grease and line the base and sides of a 20 × 30cm (8 × 12in) baking tray.

Put the butter and sugar into a large mixing bowl, or the bowl of a stand mixer, and whisk together until light and fluffy. Mix together the eggs, milk and vanilla extract in a jug, then slowly pour this into the butter and sugar mixture, whisking continuously. Once combined, sift in the flour and salt, then fold them through.

Spoon into the prepared baking tray and bake for 30–35 minutes, or until a skewer inserted comes out clean. Leave to cool completely.

To make the icing, sift the icing sugar into a bowl and add 2–3 tablespoons of water, a little at a time, until you have a thick-ish but pourable consistency. Spread the icing over the top of the cooled sponge, then sprinkle with the sprinkles! Allow to firm up for an hour before serving with custard, if you like.

Serves 12–18
–
Prep 10 mins
–
Bake 35 mins

COFFEE AND WALNUT CAKE

This classic cake perfectly epitomises a traybake which is suitable for everyday but also doubles up for special occasions. I guarantee that you know someone for whom coffee and walnut is their favourite (*cough* Dad). Instant coffee works perfectly here: you get a good, concentrated flavour without too much liquid.

250g (9oz) salted butter, at room
   temperature, plus extra for greasing
2½ tbsp instant coffee dissolved
   in 2 tbsp boiling water
50ml (3 tablespoons) milk
150g (5oz) caster (superfine) sugar
100g (3½oz) light soft brown sugar
5 eggs, beaten
200g (7oz) self-raising flour
½ tsp bicarbonate of soda (baking soda)
100g (3½oz) walnuts, ground to a
   powder in a high-speed blender
1 tsp fine salt

For the topping
200g (7oz) salted butter, at room
   temperature
400g (14oz) icing (confectioners') sugar
1½ tbsp instant coffee dissolved
   in 2 tbsp boiling water
50g (2oz) walnuts, roughly chopped

Preheat the oven to 160°C fan/180°C/350°F/Gas mark 4. Grease and line the base and sides of a 20 × 30cm (8 × 12in) baking tray.

Combine the coffee and milk in a small bowl and set aside.

Put the butter and sugars into a large mixing bowl, or the bowl of a stand mixer, and whisk together until light and fluffy. Slowly add the eggs, mixing between each addition and scraping down the sides of the bowl as you go. Sift in the flour and bicarbonate of soda, then fold through along with the walnuts and salt, followed by the coffee mixture. Mix with a large spoon until combined, then spoon into the prepared baking tray.

Bake for 35 minutes, or until a skewer inserted comes out clean. Allow to cool completely.

To make the icing, put the butter into a large mixing bowl, or the bowl of a stand mixer. Sift in the icing sugar, then add the coffee mixture. Whisk together until light and fluffy. Spread over the cooled cake and scatter with the chopped walnuts. Slice and serve.

DATE CAKE (QUEEN MOTHER'S CAKE)

This recipe is adapted from an ancient print-out my grandma always had stuck to her notice board. It proudly announced that this was the Queen Mother's favourite cake and should be sold (not given) and the money donated to a charitable organization. Whenever we make it, it reminds me of my grandma (who always reminded me a bit of the late Queen!).

150g (5oz) salted butter, at room temperature, plus extra for greasing
225g (8oz) pitted dates, chopped
1 tsp bicarbonate of soda (baking soda)
200ml (7fl oz) boiling water
225g (8oz) soft light brown sugar
2 eggs, beaten
1 tsp fine salt
1 tsp vanilla bean paste
100g (3½oz) walnuts, chopped
280g (10oz) plain (all-purpose) flour
1 tsp baking powder

For the topping
120g (4¼oz) light soft brown sugar
60g (2oz) salted butter
60g (2oz) double (heavy) cream

Preheat the oven to 160°C fan/180°C/350°F/Gas mark 4. Grease and line the base and sides of a 20 × 30cm (8 × 12in) baking tray.

Put the dates and bicarbonate of soda into a small bowl. Pour over the measured boiling water and leave to soak for 10 minutes.

Meanwhile, beat together the butter and brown sugar in a large mixing bowl. Add the eggs and beat again to combine. Mix in the salt, vanilla and chopped walnuts, before sifting in the flour and baking powder. Add the date and water mixture and mix again to completely combine.

Spoon the batter into the prepared tray and bake for 40 minutes, or until a skewer inserted comes out clean. Leave to cool.

To make the topping, combine the sugar, butter and cream in a saucepan over a medium heat. Allow the sugar and butter to melt together, stirring gently with a wooden spoon. Bring to the boil (do not stir) and let it bubble for 30 seconds. Pour over the cooled cake, then allow to set slightly before serving.

Serves 18
–
Prep 15 mins
–
Bake 40 mins

MARBLE CAKE

The best of both worlds – chocolate and vanilla – this cake comes out looking like a Friesian cow. When I discovered marble cake as a child, I thought it was the coolest-looking thing. I've topped mine with a bittersweet ganache because my trials with buttercream made it too sweet! Try washing it down with a cold glass of milk.

250g (9oz) salted butter, plus extra
    for greasing
250g (9oz) caster (superfine) sugar
5 eggs, beaten
250g (9oz) self-raising flour
135ml (4½fl oz) whole milk
1 tbsp vanilla bean paste
60g (2oz) cocoa

For the icing
150g (5oz) salted butter
200g (7oz) dark chocolate
1½ tbsp golden syrup
160ml (5½fl oz) double (heavy) cream

Preheat the oven to 160°C fan/180°C/350°F/Gas mark 4. Grease and line the base and sides of a 20 × 30cm (8 × 12in) baking tray.

Put the butter and sugar into a large mixing bowl, or the bowl of a stand mixer, and whisk until creamy and light in colour. Whisking continuously, or with the motor still running, slowly add the eggs. Sift in the flour, then add 3 tablespoons of the milk and the vanilla bean paste and fold it through. Mix until combined. In a separate mixing bowl, sift in the cocoa, then slowly add the remaining 6 tablespoons of milk to form make a paste, and then a chocolatey mixture. Add 500g (1lb 2oz) of the cake batter and carefully mix until combined.

Dot half the vanilla mixture into the base of the prepared baking tray, followed by half of the chocolate mixture, loosely alternating colours. Repeat with the remaining batter, then drag a skewer or chopstick through the mixture to create a marbled pattern. Bake for 30 minutes, or until a skewer inserted comes out clean, then allow to cool completely.

While the cake is cooking, make the ganache. Melt together the butter and chocolate in a heatproof bowl set over a pan of barely simmering water. Once melted, add the golden syrup and cream. Mix to combine. Leave to cool to room temperature; it will thicken to a spreadable consistency.

Spread the ganache all over the top of the cake using an off-set palette knife or the back of a spoon, then serve.

Serves 18
–
Prep 15 mins
–
Bake 30 mins

PISTACHIO CAKE

I still think of pistachios as the height of luxury, and order anything pistachio-flavoured when I get the chance. The ground pistachios give this sponge a moist crumb, with pops of a more intense flavour from the more coarsely-cut pistachios. Topped with a slightly tangy mascarpone frosting and beautiful homemade cherries in syrup, this is a really special bake.

210g (7½oz) butter, at room temperature, plus extra for greasing
250g (9oz) caster (superfine) sugar
5 eggs, beaten
400g (14oz) shelled pistachios, 280g (10oz) ground to a fine powder in a high-speed blender, 120g (4¼oz) roughly chopped
110g (3¾oz) self-raising flour
1 tsp flaky sea salt

For the cherries
200g (7oz) caster (superfine) sugar
250g (9oz) cherries

For the mascarpone frosting
100g (3½oz) salted butter
250g (9oz) icing (confectioners') sugar
250g (9oz) mascarpone

Preheat the oven to 160°C fan/180°C/350°F/Gas mark 4. Grease and line the base and sides of a 20 × 30cm (8 × 12in) baking tray.

Put the butter and sugar into a large mixing bowl, or the bowl of a stand mixer, and whisk together until light in colour and fully combined. Gradually add the eggs, whisking between each addition. Add the ground and chopped pistachios, then sift in the flour and salt and fold together until fully incorporated.

Spoon the batter into the prepared tray and bake for 40 minutes, or until a skewer inserted comes out clean. Leave to cool completely in its tin.

Meanwhile, prepare the cherries. Combine the sugar and 200ml (7fl oz) of water in a saucepan over a medium heat, swirling the pan gently to combine. Once the sugar has dissolved, increase the heat to high and bubble for about 4 minutes, until the mixture is lightly syrupy (do not stir). Add the cherries and continue to cook for another 3–4 minutes, turning carefully with a wooden spoon, until the syrup is thick enough to coat the cherries and is turning slightly pink. Take off the heat and allow the cherries to sit for a couple of minutes before spooning out on to a plate lined with baking parchment. Leave to cool.

When the cake and cherries are cooled, make the frosting. Add the butter to a large mixing bowl, or the bowl of a stand mixer, then sift in the icing sugar. Whisk until they have combined to form a sandy mixture. Add the mascarpone cheese and beat until fully combined, light and fluffy. Spread the frosting over the pistachio cake and dot with the cherries. Slice and serve – be careful of the cherry stones as you eat.

Serves 18
–
Prep 35 mins
–
Bake 40 mins

CHOCOLATE AND HAZELNUT CAKE

This sponge almost has a hint of chocolate chip cookie about it, with the ground, toasted hazelnuts giving a buttery warmth to the whole cake. I find chocolate hazelnut spread irresistible so all elements of this bake are a hit!

250g (9oz) salted butter, at room temperature, plus extra for greasing
150g (5oz) caster (superfine) sugar
100g (3½oz) soft light brown sugar
5 eggs, beaten
150g (5oz) self-raising flour
100g (3½oz) toasted blanched hazelnuts, coarsely ground in a high-speed blender
50ml (3 tablespoons) whole milk
2 tsp vanilla bean paste
140g (5oz) dark chocolate, cut into very fine chips

For the buttercream
300g (10½oz) icing (confectioners') sugar
150g (5oz) salted butter, at room temperature
100g (3½oz) plus 2 tablespoons chocolate hazelnut spread
1 tbsp whole or semi-skimmed milk

Preheat the oven to 160°C fan/180°C/350°F/Gas mark 4. Grease and line the base and sides of a 20 × 30cm (8 × 12in) baking tray.

Put the butter and both the sugars into a large mixing bowl, or the bowl of a stand mixer, and whisk together until light and fluffy. Whisking continuously, slowly add the eggs. Once incorporated, sift in the flour, then fold through along with the ground hazelnuts, the milk and vanilla bean paste. Mix until combined, then fold through the chocolate pieces.

Spoon the batter into the prepared baking tray, smoothing the top, and bake for 35–40 minutes, or until a skewer inserted comes out clean. Leave to cool completely.

To make the buttercream, sift the icing sugar into a large mixing bowl, or the bowl of a stand mixer, then add the butter, 100g (3½oz) of the chocolate hazelnut spread and the milk. Whisk until combined and smooth, then spread over the top of the cooled cake. Gently heat the remaining 2 tablespoons of chocolate hazelnut spread in a small saucepan over a low heat to loosen, then drizzle this over the top of the buttercream. Slice and serve.

Serves 18
–
Prep 15 mins
–
Bake 40 mins

TRES LECHES CAKE

This Mexican-inspired cake is named after the three milks (leches) which go into the making of it. The sponge becomes the perfect level of soggy, steeped in the sweetened milks. It's so sweet and decadent that you'lll want to take it slow, with a cup of tea, or perhaps an iced coffee.

butter or oil, for greasing
5 eggs, separated
250g (9oz) golden caster (superfine) sugar
120ml (4¼fl oz) plus 2 tablespoons milk
225g (8oz) plain (all-purpose) flour
1 tsp baking powder
400ml (14fl oz) evaporated milk
400g (14oz) can condensed milk
300ml (10½fl oz) double (heavy) cream
pinch of flaky sea salt

Preheat the oven to 160°C fan/180°C/350°F/Gas mark 4. Grease and line the base and sides of a 20 × 30cm (8 × 12in) baking tray.

Put the egg whites into a large bowl or the bowl of a stand mixer. Whisk until foamy – if you don't have a stand mixer, an electric whisk will make this much easier – then slowly add 175g (6oz) of the sugar, a tablespoon at a time, whisking between each addition. Continue to whisk until the mixture forms stiff peaks and looks glossy. Transfer to a clean bowl.

Add the egg yolks to the bowl you used for the egg whites (no need to clean it), along with the remaining 75g (2½oz) sugar. Whisk to ribbon stage (this means that the whisk should leave a trail when you draw it through the mixture in a figure of eight). Fold one third of the egg whites into the yolk mixture, and once combined, add another third. Pour in the 120ml (4¼fl oz) milk, then sift in the flour and baking powder and fold through to get rid of any lumps. Fold in the remaining egg whites, mixing delicately but thoroughly – you don't want to knock out the air.

Spoon the batter into the prepared tray and smooth the top. Bake for 30–35 minutes, or until a skewer inserted comes out clean. Leave to cool slightly in the tray for 15 minutes.

In a bowl, combine the evaporated milk with 300g (10½oz) of the condensed milk. Add the remaining 2 tablespoons of milk and mix to combine.

Poke lots of holes into the cake with a wooden skewer, then pour half of this milk mixture over the cake. Allow to soak in for 5 minutes, then pour over the remaining mixture. Leave to cool completely in the tin.

Pour the double cream into a (clean) mixing bowl or bowl of the stand mixer. Add the remaining 100g (3½oz) of condensed milk and a pinch of salt flakes and whisk until holding medium-soft waves, then spread over the surface of the cooled cake. Cut into squares and serve.

Serves 18
—
Prep 15 mins
—
Bake 35 mins

COCONUT AND JAM SPONGE

Another school-dinner throwback. You really can't beat the simplicity of this cake. With coconut in the sponge *and* on top, it's really flavoursome. Custard is 'optional' – but really 100 per cent obligatory. Try changing the jam for a citrus curd for a little twist on this retro cake.

250g (9oz) salted butter, at room temperature, plus extra for greasing
250g (9oz) caster (superfine) sugar
5 eggs, beaten
200g (7oz) self-raising flour
1 tsp baking powder
140g (5oz) desiccated (dried shredded) coconut
3 tbsp milk
4 tbsp strawberry or raspberry jam

custard, to serve (optional)

Preheat the oven to 160°C fan/180°C/350°F/Gas mark 4. Grease and line the base and sides of a 20 × 30cm (8 × 12in) baking tray.

Put the butter and sugar into a large mixing bowl, or the bowl of a stand mixer, and whisk together until creamy and pale in colour. Whisking continuously, slowly add the eggs. Once all are incorporated, sift in the flour and baking powder, then fold through, along with 100g (3½oz) of the desiccated coconut and the milk. Mix to combine.

Spoon the batter into the prepared baking tray. Bake for 35–40 minutes or until a skewer inserted comes out clean, then allow to cool completely.

Spread the jam all over the top of the sponge, then sprinkle with the remaining 40g (1½oz) of desiccated coconut. Serve with custard, if liked.

Serves 18
–
Prep 15 mins
–
Bake 40 mins

BROWN BUTTER AND PECAN CAKE

This is a new favourite of mine, not least for the aroma of the browned butter when you're making it: as you caramelize the proteins in the butter, it smells like digestive biscuits. Pair that with naturally buttery-tasting pecans and this is an instant win.

For the browned butter
300g (10½oz) salted butter

For the butter-and-pecan base
80g (3oz) salted butter, plus extra
   for greasing
80g (3oz) soft light brown sugar
200g (7oz) pecans, roughly chopped

For the sponge
250g (9oz) light soft brown sugar
5 eggs, beaten
200g (7oz) self-raising flour
1 tsp baking powder
1 tsp flaky sea salt
100g (3½oz) pecans, ground to a
   powder in a high-speed blender

whipped cream, to serve

Begin by making the browned butter. Put the butter into a saucepan over a medium heat. Let the butter melt, then continue to cook until the white flecks in the butter are starting to turn golden. Continue until the flecks become a darker brown (like almond skins). The butter will foam, and the foam will turn orangey brown. Weigh the browned butter into a mixing bowl – it should come to about 250g (9oz). Set aside to cool for 20 minutes.

Meanwhile, grease and line the base and sides of a 20 × 30cm (8 × 12in) baking tray. Then, to make the butter-and-pecan base, combine the butter and sugar in a small bowl. Smooth this mixture across the base of the prepared baking tray, then scatter with the chopped pecans.

Preheat the oven to 160°C fan/180°C/350°F/Gas mark 4.

To make the sponge, put the sugar into a large mixing bowl, or the bowl of a stand mixer, and stir in the cooled browned butter. Add the eggs and whisk until thickened and pale. Sift in the flour and baking powder, fold through the salt and ground pecans. Mix until combined.

Pour the batter over the pecan base and bake for 40–45 minutes, or until a skewer inserted comes out clean.

Let the cake cool in its tin for 20 minutes before turning out on to a wire rack. Serve warm, with whipped cream.

Serves 18
–
Prep 10 mins
–
Bake 45 mins

Comforting Sponges

CHOCOLATE AND GUINNESS CAKE

This one is definitely popular for a reason. The flavour of the Guinness transforms as the cake bakes, creating an amazingly fudgy sponge. Topped with the pillowy, extra-creamy cream cheese topping, it's dangerously easy to eat.

250g (9oz) salted butter, cut into chunks, plus extra for greasing
250ml (8¾fl oz) Guinness
200g (7oz) caster (superfine) sugar
200g (7oz) soft light brown sugar
80g (3oz) cocoa powder
280g (10oz) plain (all-purpose) flour
1 tbsp bicarbonate of soda (baking soda)
150g (5½oz) soured cream
3 eggs, beaten
2 tsp vanilla bean paste

For the frosting
100g (3½oz) salted butter, at room temperature
200g (7oz) icing (confectioners') sugar
300g (10½oz) full-fat soft cream cheese
50ml (3 tablespoons) double (heavy) cream
1 tsp vanilla bean paste

Preheat the oven to 160°C fan/180°C/350°F/Gas mark 4. Grease and line the base and sides of a 20 × 30cm (8 × 12in) baking tray.

Put the Guinness and butter into a saucepan over a low heat until just melted. Set aside.

In a large mixing bowl, combine the sugars, then sift in the cocoa powder, flour and bicarbonate of soda. Mix to combine. In a jug, mix together the soured cream, eggs and vanilla bean paste. Mix the Guinness and butter mixture into the dry ingredients using a balloon whisk, then beat in the eggs and soured cream mixture.

Pour the batter into the prepared baking tray and bake for 40–45 minutes, or until a skewer inserted comes out clean. Allow to cool completely in the tin.

To make the frosting, put the butter into a large bowl, or the bowl of a stand mixer, and whisk until softened and creamy. Sift in the icing sugar, then add the cream cheese and whisk again until smooth. Add the double cream and vanilla and beat briefly to combine, then spoon on to the top of the cooled cake before slicing and serving.

Serves 18
–
Prep 15 mins
–
Bake 45 mins

CARROT CAKE

This is a firm family favourite that has been perfected over the years. It always ranks high on my birthday cake request list – and I have been known to scrape extra cream cheese frosting onto my plate because it's my favourite bit. Made with oil instead of butter, this is a very easy recipe to pull together, with a very simple method, so there's no excuse not to give it a go.

200ml (7fl oz) sunflower oil, plus extra for greasing
300g (10½oz) light soft brown sugar
1 tbsp ground cinnamon
1 tsp ground ginger
250g (9oz) plain (all-purpose) flour
2 tsp baking powder
2 tsp bicarbonate of soda (baking soda)
½ tsp fine salt
360g (12½oz) grated peeled carrots
4 eggs, beaten
50g (2oz) chopped walnuts, plus extra to serve (optional)

For the frosting
140g (5oz) full-fat cream cheese
70g (2¼oz) salted butter, at room temperature
300g (10½oz) icing (confectioners') sugar

Preheat the oven to 160°C fan/180°C/350°F/Gas mark 4. Grease and line the base and sides of a 20 × 30cm (8 × 12in) baking tray.

Combine the sugar and ground spices in a large bowl, then sift in the flour, baking powder, bicarbonate of soda and salt. Mix together the sunflower oil, grated carrots and eggs in a large jug or separate bowl and stir into the dry mixture, combining thoroughly to get rid of any pockets of flour. Stir through the walnuts, then spoon into the prepared baking tray.

Bake for 45–50 minutes, or until a skewer inserted comes out clean. Leave to cool.

To make the frosting, put the cream cheese and butter in a large mixing bowl, or the bowl of a stand mixer, then sift in the icing sugar and whisk briefly to combine. Smooth the frosting over the cooled cake, scatter with extra chopped walnuts, if liked, then slice and serve.

Serves 18
–
Prep 15 mins
–
Bake 50 mins

Comforting Sponges

BROWNIES AND BLONDIES

Eight deliciously moreish, chocolate-based fudgy slabs, ranging from S'mores Brownies to Gingerbread Blondies. My desired end result for all of these recipes is truffle-like decadence – so you'll find no cakiness in this chapter. The key to getting that texture? Use the fridge! The brownies might seem on the wobbly side when you get them out the oven, but after a few hours or a night (if you can wait that long) in the fridge, the middle will set like ganache. Dreamy.

CHOCOLATE ORANGE BROWNIES

This is my most classic recipe, with minimal frill (apart from the zest), so it can be your gateway into being a brownie boss. Chocolate and orange is a combination that shouldn't just be left for Christmas (I love it all year round) — but if you're not a fan, just leave it out, and you'll have perfect, madly chocolatey brownies instead.

250g (9oz) salted butter, roughly cubed, plus extra for greasing
250g (9oz) dark chocolate, broken into pieces
4 eggs, beaten
200g (7oz) caster (superfine) sugar
150g (5½oz) light soft brown sugar
120g (4¼oz) plain (all-purpose) flour
40g (1½oz) cocoa powder
zest of 3 oranges
200g (7oz) milk chocolate, cut into rough 1cm (½in) chunks
1 tsp flaky sea salt

Preheat the oven to 160°C fan/180°C/350°F/Gas mark 4. Grease and line the base and sides of a 20 × 30cm (8 × 12in) baking tray.

Combine the butter and chocolate in a heatproof bowl set over a pan of barely simmering water and gently heat until melted (if you prefer, you can do this in short bursts in the microwave, stirring between each one). Stir together until smooth, then set aside to cool slightly.

Put the eggs and both types of sugar in a large mixing bowl, or the bowl of a stand mixer, and whisk until thick and pale in colour (about 8–10 minutes by hand, or 3–4 minutes using a stand mixer). Pour in the butter and chocolate mixture, and whisk until just combined. Sift in the flour and cocoa powder, then add the orange zest, milk chocolate chunks and salt. Fold together and mix until just combined.

Spoon into the prepared baking tray and bake for 20 minutes, or until the top has a set, golden crust, and there's still a slight wobble in the very middle of the tin. Allow to cool to room temperature, then chill in the fridge for a few hours or overnight before slicing and serving (this will ensure very fudgy brownies).

Serves 18–24

—

Prep 20 mins, plus chilling

—

Bake 20 mins

HAZELNUT AND SOUR CHERRY BROWNIES

This recipe is my answer to 'fruit and nut'. With little hits of sweet and sour fruit and a warm, nutty crunch, they're pretty straightforward but utterly delicious. You don't need to worry about the nuts catching as they're nestled in the batter – neat. I dare anyone to eat just one.

260g (9¼oz) salted butter, roughly cubed, plus extra for greasing
200g (7oz) blanched hazelnuts
475g (1lb 1oz) dark chocolate, broken into pieces
4 eggs, beaten
330g (11½oz) soft dark brown sugar
70g (2¼oz) self-raising flour
1 tsp flaky sea salt
225g (8oz) dried cherries, roughly chopped

Preheat the oven to 170°C fan/190°C/375°F/Gas mark 5. Grease and line the base and sides of a 20 × 30cm (8 × 12in) baking tray.

Tip the hazelnuts on to a baking sheet and roast for 6–8 minutes. Leave to cool, then roughly chop.

Combine the chocolate and butter in a heatproof bowl set over a pan of barely simmering water and gently heat until melted (if you prefer, you can do this in short bursts in the microwave, stirring between each one). Stir together until smooth, then set aside to cool slightly.

Put the eggs and sugar into a large mixing bowl, or the bowl of a stand mixer, and whisk until thick and pale in colour (about 8–10 minutes by hand, or 3–4 minutes using a stand mixer). Pour in the butter and chocolate mixture, and whisk until just combined, then sift in the flour. Fold through, along with the salt, dried cherries and chopped hazelnuts. Mix until combined.

Spoon into the prepared baking tray and bake for 25–30 minutes, or until the top has a papery crust all over and there's little to no wobble in the mixture. Allow to cool to room temperature, then chill in the fridge for a few hours or overnight before slicing and serving (this will ensure very fudgy brownies).

Serves 18–24
–
Prep 20 mins, plus chilling
–
Bake 38 mins

COOKIE DOUGH BROWNIES

I can't resist sampling uncooked cookie dough when I'm baking – particularly if it has chocolate chips in – and with this, you end up with a happy medium: soft dough, on the verge of being underdone, surrounded by fudgy brownie. Pass me the ice cream! I tried these before they were chilled in the fridge, so can testify that they're the bomb, hot or cold. I would even advocate serving them 10 minutes after they come out the oven, scooped from the tin and piled with dairy.

For the cookie dough

150g (5½oz) salted butter, at room temperature, plus extra for greasing
200g (7oz) soft light brown sugar
1 egg
1 tsp vanilla extract
160g (5¾oz) plain (all-purpose) flour
1 tsp baking powder
150g (5½oz) chocolate chips (a combination of milk, dark and white chocolate is fun)

For the brownie mixture

250g (9oz) salted butter, roughly cubed
250g (9oz) dark chocolate, broken into pieces
4 eggs, beaten
200g (7oz) caster (superfine) sugar
150g (5oz) light soft brown sugar
120g (4¼oz) plain (all-purpose) flour,
40g (1½oz) cocoa powder
150g (5½oz) milk, white or blonde chocolate chunks
1 tsp flaky sea salt

Preheat the oven to 160°C fan/180°C/350°F/Gas mark 4. Grease and line the base and sides of a 20 × 30cm (8 × 12in) baking tray.

Start by making the cookie dough. In a large bowl, cream together the butter and sugar with a wooden spoon, then stir in the egg and vanilla. Sift in the flour and baking powder and mix until just combined, then stir through the chocolate chips. Form into heaped 1-teaspoon balls and place on a plate. Refrigerate briefly while you make the brownie mixture.

For the brownie batter, melt the butter and dark chocolate together in a heatproof bowl set over a pan of barely simmering water (if you prefer, you can do this in short bursts in the microwave, stirring between each one). Mix together until smooth, then set aside to cool slightly.

Put the eggs and both sugars into a large mixing bowl, or the bowl of a stand mixer, and whisk until thick and pale in colour (about 8–10 minutes by hand, or 3–4 minutes using a stand mixer). Pour in the butter and chocolate mixture, and whisk until just combined. Sift in the flour and cocoa, then add the chocolate chunks and flaky sea salt. Fold together with a large metal spoon and mix until just combined. Spoon into the prepared baking tray. Take the cookie dough balls out of the fridge (rolling them into smoother balls if they're a bit scraggy) and place them randomly on the brownie mixture, leaving gaps between them.

Bake for 20–25 minutes, or until the top has a set, golden crust, but there's still a slight wobble in the very middle of the tray. Allow to cool to room temperature, then chill in the fridge for a few hours or overnight before slicing and serving (this will ensure very fudgy brownies).

Serves 24
–
Prep 25 mins, plus chilling
–
Bake 25 mins

S'MORES BROWNIES

Biscuit base, brownie, charred marshmallow. Phwoar. This has all the charm of the American campfire biscuit sandwich, without the need to smell like smoke. The marshmallows are layered onto the warm brownies so that they melt on, before their sleepover in the fridge. A moment under the grill, or a blowtorch for a pyrotechnic display, and the American dream is complete.

For the base
300g (10½oz) digestive biscuits, crushed to a fine crumb
100g (3½oz) salted butter, melted

For the brownies
200g (7oz) salted butter, roughly cubed, plus extra for greasing
200g (7oz) dark chocolate, broken into pieces
150g (5½oz) milk chocolate, broken into pieces
3 eggs, beaten
250g (9oz) soft light brown sugar
50g (2oz) self-raising flour
1 tsp flaky sea salt
540g (1lb 3½oz) medium-sized marshmallows

Preheat the oven to 160°C fan/180°C/350°F/Gas mark 4. Grease and line the base and sides of a 20 × 30cm (8 × 12in) baking tray.

Begin by making the base. Combine the crushed digestives and melted butter in bowl until thoroughly mixed, then pour into the base of the prepared tray, pushing down with the back of a spoon until nicely compacted. Bake for 10 minutes.

Meanwhile, prepare the brownie. Melt both types of chocolate and the butter together in a heatproof bowl set over a pan of barely simmering water (if you prefer, you can do this in short bursts in the microwave, stirring between each one). Mix to a smooth sauce and set aside to cool.

Put the eggs and sugar into a large mixing bowl, or the bowl of a stand mixer, and whisk until thick and pale in colour (about 8–10 minutes by hand, or 3–4 minutes using a stand mixer). Pour in the chocolate and butter mixture, and whisk until just combined. Sift in the flour, then add the flaky sea salt. Fold together with a large metal spoon and mix until just combined.

Remove the baking tray from the oven and spoon the brownie mixture over the base. Bake for 20–25 minutes, or until the top is papery and the brownie mixture only has a slight wobble left in the middle.

Remove from the oven and arrange the marshmallows on top of the brownie, packing them in so that they cover the whole thing. They should fuse to the brownie due to the residual heat. Cool to room temperature, then refrigerate for a few hours or overnight (this will ensure very fudgy brownies).

The next day, preheat the grill (broiler) to high. Trim any baking parchment that might be sticking out of the baking tray, then pop under the grill for a few minutes, or until toasted and golden, with the tips of the marshmallows beginning to char. Keep a close eye to ensure they don't burn. (Alternatively, carefully use a kitchen blowtorch.) Slice and serve.

Serves 24
–
Prep 25 mins, plus chilling
–
Bake 25 mins

CHOCOLATE PEANUT BUTTER BROWNIES

I resisted the urge to spoon jam through this, too, but that gauntlet can be for your experimentation. Salty chopped peanuts with a smooth nutty marbling on top? These are irresistible.

250g (9oz) salted butter, roughly cubed, plus extra for greasing
250g (9oz) dark chocolate, broken into pieces
4 eggs, beaten
100g (3½oz) caster (superfine) sugar
250g (9oz) light soft brown sugar
120g (4¼oz) plain (all-purpose) flour
40g (1½oz) cocoa powder
100g (3½oz) salted peanuts, roughly chopped
200g (7oz) runny, smooth peanut butter

Preheat the oven to 160°C fan/180°C/350°F/Gas mark 4. Grease and line the base and sides of a 20 × 30cm (8 × 12in) baking tray.

Melt the butter and chocolate together in a heatproof bowl set over a pan of barely simmering water (if you prefer, you can do this in short bursts in the microwave, stirring between each one). Stir until smooth, then set aside to cool slightly.

Put the eggs and both types of sugar into a large mixing bowl, or the bowl of a stand mixer, and whisk until thick and pale in colour (about 8–10 minutes by hand, or 3–4 minutes using a stand mixer). Pour in the butter and chocolate mixture, and whisk until just combined. Sift in the flour and cocoa, then stir through the peanuts. Fold it all together with a large spoon and mix until just combined. Spoon into the prepared baking tray. Dot the peanut butter on top, then use a skewer to swirl it through for a marbled effect.

Bake for 20 minutes, or until the top has a set, golden crust, but there's still a slight wobble in the very middle. Allow to cool to room temperature, then chill in the fridge for a few hours or overnight (this will ensure very fudgy brownies).

Serves 24
–
Prep 15 mins, plus chilling
–
Bake 20 mins

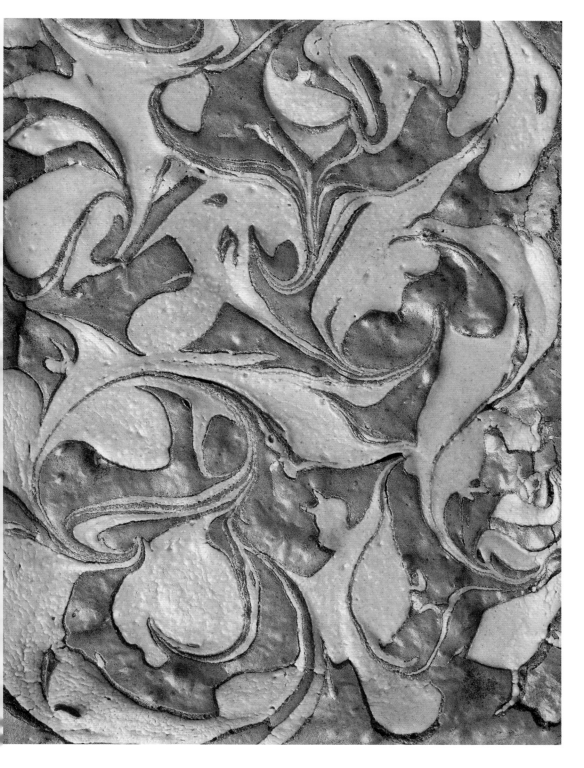

COFFEE CHEESECAKE BROWNIES

I'm not actually a mad fan of cheesecake, but here I've struck a fine balance. The coffee manages to give these brownies a mocha vibe, with the creamy cheesecake element providing the means of marbling – and I'm pretty proud of the end result.

260g (9¼oz) salted butter, roughly cubed, plus extra for greasing
475g (1lb 1oz) dark chocolate, broken into pieces
2 tbsp instant coffee
4 eggs, beaten
330g (11oz) soft light brown sugar
70g (2¼oz) self-raising flour
1 tsp flaky sea salt

For the cheesecake
1 tbsp instant coffee
½ tbsp boiling water
150g (5½oz) full-fat cream cheese
50g (2oz) caster (superfine) sugar
1 egg, beaten
1 tbsp plain (all-purpose) flour

Preheat the oven to 170°C fan/190°C/375°F/Gas mark 5. Grease and line the base and sides of a 20 × 30cm (8 × 12in) baking tray.

Melt the chocolate and butter in a heatproof bowl set over a pan of barely simmering water (if you prefer, you can do this in short bursts in the microwave, stirring between each one). Mix to form a smooth sauce, then stir through the instant coffee and set aside to cool.

Put the eggs and sugar in a large mixing bowl, or the bowl of a stand mixer, and whisk until thick and pale in colour (about 8–10 minutes by hand, or 3–4 minutes using a stand mixer). Pour in the butter and chocolate mixture, and whisk until just combined, then sift in the flour and fold through. Stir in the salt, then spoon the batter into the prepared tray.

Now prepare the cheesecake mixture. In a separate bowl, combine the instant coffee with the boiling water and stir to dissolve. Add the cream cheese, sugar, egg and flour, and use a balloon whisk to gently beat it all together.

Use the back of a tablespoon to make dents in the brownie mixture, and spoon the cheesecake mixture into these spaces. Swirl through the brownie mixture with a skewer for a marbled effect.

Bake for 25 minutes, or until the top has a crust and only a slight wobble remains in the middle. Allow to cool to room temperature, then chill in the fridge for a few hours or overnight before slicing and serving (this will ensure very fudgy brownies).

Serves 24
–
Prep 25 mins, plus chilling
–
Bake 25 mins

ALMOND BUTTER AND CARAMELIZED CHOCOLATE BLONDIES

Runny nut butters are one of my favourite things, and thank you, 2020s, for making caramelized white chocolate so popular. Here, the twice-caramelized chocolate becomes almost fudgy, buried in the batter and nestled around the subtle sweetness of the almond butter.

250g (9oz) salted butter, roughly cubed, plus extra for greasing
250g (9oz) white chocolate, broken into pieces
150g (5½oz) golden caster (superfine) sugar
150g (5½oz) soft light brown sugar
4 eggs, beaten
250g (9oz) plain (all-purpose) flour
½ tsp flaky sea salt
300g (10½oz) blonde chocolate, cut into rough 1cm (½in) chunks
170g (6oz) smooth almond butter

Preheat the oven to 160°C fan/180°C/350°F/Gas mark 4. Grease and line the base and sides of a 20 × 30cm (8 × 12in) baking tray.

Melt the butter and white chocolate together in a heatproof bowl set over a pan of barely simmering water (if you prefer, you can do this in short bursts in the microwave, stirring between each one). Set aside to cool slightly for 5 minutes.

Put both types of sugar and the eggs into a large mixing bowl, or the bowl of a stand mixer, and whisk until thick and pale in colour (about 8–10 minutes by hand, or 3–4 minutes using a stand mixer). Pour in the butter and chocolate mixture, and whisk until just combined. Sift in the flour, then add the flaky sea salt and blonde chocolate chunks and fold through. Spoon the batter into the prepared tray. Dot the almond butter on top, then drag a skewer through the blobs to create a marbled effect.

Bake for 35 minutes, or until the top has a golden crust. Allow to cool to room temperature, then chill in the fridge for a few hours or overnight before slicing and serving (this will ensure very fudgy brownies).

Serves 24
–
Prep 25 mins, plus chilling
–
Bake 35 mins

GINGERBREAD BLONDIES

These blondies have a wintry undertone with all their delicious spices! The broken-up ginger biscuits melt into the mixture to become little gingery bites.

250g (9oz) salted butter, roughly cubed, plus extra for greasing
250g (9oz) white chocolate, broken into pieces
150g (5½oz) golden caster (superfine) sugar
150g (5½oz) light muscovado sugar
4 eggs, beaten
250g (9oz) plain (all-purpose) flour
1 tbsp ground ginger
2 tsp ground cinnamon
¼ tsp ground mixed spice
150g (5½oz) ginger biscuits, broken into pieces

Preheat the oven to 160°C fan/180°C/350°F/Gas mark 4. Grease and line the base and sides of a 20 × 30cm (8 × 12in) baking tray.

Melt the butter and white chocolate together in a heatproof bowl set over a pan of barely simmering water (if you prefer, you can do this in short bursts in the microwave, stirring between each one). Set aside to cool slightly for 5 minutes.

Put both types of sugar and the eggs into a large mixing bowl, or the bowl of a stand mixer, and whisk until thick and pale in colour (about 8–10 minutes by hand, or 3–4 minutes using a stand mixer). Pour in the butter and chocolate mixture, and whisk until just combined. Sift in the flour and the spices, then add the broken biscuits and fold through. Spoon the batter into the prepared tray, then bake for 30–35 minutes, or until the top has a golden crust.

Allow to cool to room temperature, then chill in the fridge for a few hours or overnight before slicing and serving (this will ensure very fudgy brownies).

Serves 24
–
Prep 20 mins, plus chilling
–
Bake 35 mins

PASTRY

In this chapter, I've given foolproof instructions for making your own pastry, but you can always buy a block of shop-bought if making your own is too intimidating a prospect. I recommend a 500g (1lb 2oz) block rather than using ready-rolled, as pre-rolled pastry has a tendency to shrink and wouldn't fit the dimensions of our tin. It's important to blind bake your pastry (using baking beads, which are readily available online or in homeware stores) to give it a headstart on cooking before you add all your delicious pie fillings.

CHERRY BAKEWELL TART

Crisp pastry, tart cherry jam and a rich almondy sponge – this is a perfectly balanced combination of flavours and textures.

For the shortcrust pastry (or use a 500g/1lb 2oz ready-made block)

360g (12½oz) plain (all-purpose) flour, plus extra for dusting
180g (6¼oz) cold unsalted butter, diced into rough 1cm (½in) cubes, plus extra for greasing
4–5 tbsp ice-cold water

For the filling

225g (8oz) caster (superfine) sugar
225g (8oz) unsalted butter, at room temperature
4 eggs, beaten
175g (6oz) ground almonds
50g (2oz) self-raising flour
340g (12oz) cherry jam
30g (1oz) flaked almonds

To finish

100g (3½oz) icing (confectioners') sugar

Begin by making the pastry. Sift the flour into a bowl, then rub in the butter using your fingertips. Stir through the water with a cutlery knife. (Alternatively, if you have a food processor, pulse the flour, then add the butter and pulse until a sandy mixture forms. Tip this into a bowl, then add 4 tablespoons of the cold water and stir through with a cutlery knife, adding the remaining water as necessary.) Form the dough into a disc, then wrap in cling film (plastic wrap). Refrigerate for 30 minutes.

Preheat the oven to 180°C fan/200°C/400°F/Gas mark 6 and place a large baking sheet inside to preheat. Grease the base and sides of a 20 × 30cm (8 × 12in) baking tray.

When the pastry has chilled, roll it out on a lightly floured surface to form a rectangle measuring about 26 × 36cm (10 × 14in). Gently ease the pastry into the prepared tray. Scrunch up a rectangle of baking parchment to soften it, then lay it over the pastry and fill with baking beads. Place the baking tray on the preheated baking sheet and blind-bake for 15 minutes, then remove the beads and parchment and bake the pastry case for another 10 minutes.

Leave to cool slightly while you make the frangipane. Reduce the oven temperature to 160°C fan/180°C/350°F/Gas mark 4.

Put the butter and sugar into a large mixing bowl, or the bowl of a stand mixer, and whisk until pale and fluffy. Whisking continuously, or with the motor still running, slowly add the eggs. Once the eggs are incorporated, fold through the ground almonds and flour.

Spread the jam on to the base of the pastry case, spoon the frangipane on top (it's easier to dollop on lumps of mixture with a big spoon, then smooth them together), then scatter with the flaked almonds. Bake for 35–40 minutes, or until the frangipane is risen and golden, and a skewer inserted into the top comes out clean. Allow to cool completely.

Sift the icing sugar into a bowl, then add 1 tablespoon of water. Mix to make a thick drizzle, then spoon this over the top in lines.

Serves 18–24

–

Prep 15 mins, plus chilling

–

Bake 65 mins

Pastry

APPLE CRUMBLE PIE

I do think crumble can make everything taste better – and giving an apple crumble a pastry base is a pretty nice detour into dessert. It can be sectioned up much more easily and neatly, while ticking all the same comfort boxes.

For the shortcrust pastry (or use a 500g/1lb 2oz ready-made block)
360g (12½oz) plain (all-purpose) flour, plus extra for dusting
180g (6¼oz) cold unsalted butter, diced into rough 1cm (½in) cubes, plus extra for greasing
4–5 tbsp ice-cold water

For the apple filling
900g–1kg (2lb–2lb 4oz) Bramley apples, peeled, cored and roughly diced
2 tbsp light soft brown sugar
3 balls stem ginger in syrup, balls finely diced, syrup reserved

For the crumble topping
300g (10½oz) plain (all-purpose) flour
125g (4½oz) light soft brown sugar
50g (2oz) demerara sugar, plus 2 tbsp to finish
190g (6¾oz) salted butter, cold and diced into rough 1cm (½in) cubes
2 tbsp stem ginger syrup (from filling, above)

custard, cream or ice cream, to serve

Make the shortcrust pastry dough following the instructions on page 89. Form the dough into a disc, then wrap in cling film (plastic wrap). Refrigerate for 30 minutes.

Preheat the oven to 180°C fan/200°C/400°F/Gas mark 6 and place a large baking sheet inside to preheat. Grease the base and sides of a 20 × 30cm (8 × 12in) baking tray.

When the pastry has chilled, roll it out on a lightly floured surface to form a rectangle measuring about 24 × 34cm (10 × 13in). Gently ease the pastry into the prepared tray. Scrunch a rectangle of baking parchment to soften it, then lay it over the pastry and fill with baking beads. Place the baking tray on the preheated baking sheet and blind-bake for 15 minutes, then remove the beads and parchment and bake the pastry crust for another 10 minutes.

Meanwhile, prepare the apple filling. Combine the apples and sugar in a saucepan, and stir through 1 tablespoon water and the chopped ginger. Place over a gentle heat for 5 minutes until the apples are slightly softened. Leave to cool for a minute while you make the crumble topping.

Combine the flour and sugars in a bowl. Add the butter and rub it in with your fingertips until you have a sandy mixture with some bigger buttery pieces. Stir through the ginger syrup.

Spoon the apple mixture into the baked tart case, then scatter the crumble on top. Scatter over the final 2 tablespoons demerara sugar. Return to the preheated baking tray in the oven and bake for 20 minutes, or until golden. Serve with custard, cream or ice cream.

Serves 12
–
Prep 20 mins, plus chilling
–
Bake 45 mins

Pastry

TREACLE TART

There's a lot to be said for a tart that is so sweet it makes your cheeks scrunch up. Made slightly less saccharine by a bit of ginger and lemon zest, this pie is great with a big blob of clotted cream or ice cream.

For the shortcrust pastry (or use a 500g/1lb 2oz ready-made block)

360g (12½oz) plain (all-purpose) flour, plus extra for dusting
180g (6¼oz) cold unsalted butter, diced into rough 1cm (½in) cubes, plus extra for greasing
4–5 tbsp ice-cold water

For the treacle filling

650g (1lb 7oz) golden syrup
zest of 1 lemon
1 tsp ground ginger
200g (7oz) fine, fresh white breadcrumbs

clotted cream or ice cream, to serve

Make the shortcrust pastry dough following the instructions on page 89. Form the dough into a disc, then wrap in cling film (plastic wrap). Refrigerate for 30 minutes.

Preheat the oven to 180°C fan/200°C/400°F/Gas mark 6 and place a large baking sheet inside to preheat. Grease the base and sides of a 20 × 30cm (8 × 12in) baking tray.

When the pastry has chilled, roll it out on a lightly floured surface to form a rectangle measuring about 24 × 34cm (10 × 13in). Gently ease the pastry into the prepared tray. Scrunch a rectangle baking parchment to soften it, then lay it over the pastry and fill with baking beads. Place the baking tray on the preheated baking sheet and blind-bake for 15 minutes, then remove the beads and parchment and bake the pastry crust for another 10 minutes.

Meanwhile, heat the golden syrup in a saucepan over a low heat to melt. Remove from the heat and stir through the lemon zest, ginger and breadcrumbs, then leave for 5 minutes for the breadcrumbs to plump up.

Remove the pastry case from the oven and reduce the temperature to 160°C fan/180°C/350°F/Gas mark 4. Spoon the breadcrumb mixture into the pastry case, then return to the preheated baking tray and bake for 35–40 minutes, or until golden and lightly firm. Slice while still warm and serve with clotted cream or ice cream.

Serves 15–20
–
Prep 20 mins, plus chilling
–
Bake 65 mins

JAM LATTICE TART

This is as simple as tarts can get, relying on the sweetness of your jam (which gets jammier as it bakes) and a lovely buttery pastry. It gives me a real feeling of nostalgia for my grandma's baking.

For the pastry (or use a 500g/1lb 2oz ready-made block)
110g (3¾oz) icing (confectioners') sugar
500g (1lb 1½oz) plain (all-purpose) flour, plus extra for dusting
280g (9¾oz) cold unsalted butter, diced into rough 1cm (½in) cubes, plus extra for greasing
6–7 tbsp ice-cold water

For the filling
370g (13oz) raspberry jam

custard, to serve (optional)

Begin by making the pastry. Sift the icing sugar and flour into a bowl, then rub in the butter using your fingertips. Stir through the water with a cutlery knife. (Alternatively, if you have a food processor, pulse the icing sugar and flour, then add the butter and pulse until a sandy mixture forms. Add 6 tablespoons of the cold water and stir through with a cutlery knife, adding the remaining water as necessary.) Remove a third of dough and form it into a small disc, then wrap in cling film (plastic wrap). Form the rest into a larger disc and wrap this in cling film too. Refrigerate both for 30 minutes.

Preheat the oven to 180°C fan/200°C/400°F/Gas mark 6 and place a large baking sheet inside to preheat. Grease the base and sides of a 20 × 30cm (8 × 12in) baking tray.

When the pastry has chilled, roll out the larger piece on a lightly floured surface to form a rectangle measuring about 24 × 34cm (10 × 13in). Gently ease the pastry into the prepared tray. Scrunch a rectangle of baking parchment to soften it, then lay it over the pastry and fill with baking beads. Place the baking tray on the preheated baking sheet and blind-bake for 15 minutes, then remove the beads and parchment and bake the pastry crust for another 5 minutes.

While the pastry crust is cooking, prepare the lattice. Roll out the remaining dough into a 20 × 30cm (8 × 12in) rectangle and slice it into roughly 1.5cm (¾in) strips (alternatively, use a lattice roller). Arrange the pastry strips on a sheet of baking parchment and weave them in and out of one another to create a lattice effect. Chill the lattice for 10 minutes.

Remove the pastry crust from the oven and spoon in the jam. Carefully slide the lattice on top of the jam filling and pinch the raw pastry on to the blind-baked sides. Return to the preheated tray and bake for another 20–25 minutes, or until golden. Serve with custard, if you like.

Serves 18–24
–
Prep 20 mins, plus chilling
–
Bake 45 mins

CUSTARD TART

This custard is my vague (and much more simplified) nod to Portuguese pastel de nata. I've definitely had my fair share of the real thing, but my version uses a rough puff pastry and a much more foolproof baked custard. Then it's over to you for the finishing flourish!

For the rough-puff pastry (or use a 500g/1lb 2oz ready-made block)

360g (12½oz) plain (all-purpose) flour, plus extra for dusting

270g (9½oz) cold unsalted butter, diced into rough 1cm (½in) cubes, plus extra for greasing

180ml (6fl oz) ice-cold water

For the custard filling

320ml (11¼fl oz) double (heavy) cream

320ml (11¼fl oz) whole milk

1 tsp vanilla bean paste

8 egg yolks (why not save the egg whites for the lemon meringue pie, overleaf?)

120g (4¼oz) caster (superfine) sugar

To serve

1 tbsp icing (confectioners') sugar

½ tsp ground cinnamon

or

2 tbsp caster (superfine) sugar

Tip the flour into a large bowl, then add the butter. Using your fingertips, gently rub the butter into the flour, leaving some large flakes of butter. Stir through the cold water using a cutlery knife, then turn out the dough on to a lightly floured surface, before forming it into a rough disc. Wrap in cling film (plastic wrap) and chill for 15 minutes.

Roll out the dough on a lightly floured surface to form a rectangle measuring roughly 15 × 40cm (6 × 15¾in). With the pastry in portrait orientation, fold the bottom third over the middle third, then the top third over that (like folding a letter). Turn the rectangle 90 degrees to the left (from landscape to portrait) and repeat the process of rolling and folding. Wrap the dough in cling film and chill for 15 minutes. Roll out, fold and chill twice more. Meanwhile, preheat the oven to 180°C fan/ 200°C/400°F/Gas mark 6. Grease the base and sides of a 20 × 30cm (8 × 12in) baking tray.

Roll out the chilled dough on a lightly floured surface to form a rectangle measuring about 24 × 34cm (10 × 13in). Carefully drape the pastry over your rolling pin, then ease it into the prepared tray, gently pushing it into the corners and 2cm (¾in) up the sides. Scrunch up a rectangle of baking parchment to soften it, then lay it over the pastry and fill with baking beads. Blind-bake for 20 minutes, then remove the beads and parchment and bake the pastry case for another 10 minutes.

Meanwhile, prepare the custard. Combine the cream, milk and vanilla in a saucepan over a low heat until steaming. Whisk the egg yolks and sugar in a bowl. Pour the warm cream mixture over the egg mixture, whisking constantly. Return to the cleaned pan and increase the heat to low–medium. Cook, stirring constantly, until the custard is thick enough to coat the back of a wooden spoon. Sieve (strain) into a bowl and leave to cool.

When the pastry case has finished cooking, remove it from the oven and reduce the oven temperature to 160°C fan/ 180°C/350°F/Gas mark 4. Push down any air bubbles in the pastry with the back of a spoon, then pour the custard into the case. Return to the oven and bake for 15–20 minutes, or until the custard has only a small wobble left in it.

Allow to cool to room temperature before serving. To serve, dust with a combination of icing sugar and cinnamon, or scatter over the caster sugar and brûlée with a kitchen blowtorch.

Serves 16

–

Prep 30 mins, plus chilling

–

Bake 50 mins

LEMON MERINGUE PIE

Shop-bought curd, topped with robust meringue, makes this a much less daunting task than it might otherwise be! With its citrussy freshness, it's the perfect dessert for when you fancy something sweet but light and refreshing.

For the shortcrust pastry (or use a 500g/1lb 2oz ready-made block)
360g (12½oz) plain (all-purpose) flour, plus extra for dusting
180g (6¼oz) cold unsalted butter, diced into rough 1cm (½in) cubes, plus extra for greasing
4–5 tbsp ice-cold water

For the meringue
5 egg whites
250g (9oz) caster (superfine) sugar
1 tbsp cornflour (cornstarch)

For the filling
480g (1lb 1oz) lemon curd

Make the shortcrust pastry dough following the instructions on page 89. Form the dough into a disc, then wrap in cling film (plastic wrap). Refrigerate for 30 minutes.

Preheat the oven to 180°C fan/200°C/400°F/Gas mark 6 and place a large baking sheet inside to preheat. Grease the base and sides of a 20 × 30cm (8 × 12in) baking tray.

When the pastry has chilled, roll it out on a lightly floured surface to form a rectangle measuring about 24 × 34cm (10 × 13in). Gently ease the pastry into the prepared tray. Scrunch up a rectangle of baking parchment to soften it, then lay it over the pastry and fill with baking beads. Place the baking tray on the preheated baking sheet and blind-bake for 15 minutes, then remove the beads and parchment and bake the pastry case for another 10 minutes.

Meanwhile, make the meringue. Put the egg whites into a large bowl or the bowl of a stand mixer. Whisk until soft peaks form – if you don't have a stand mixer, an electric whisk will make this much easier – then add the sugar, a tablespoon at a time, whisking between each addition until the mixture is thick and glossy. Whisk through the cornflour.

Remove the baked pastry case from the oven and reduce the oven temperature to 160°C fan/180°C/350°F/Gas mark 4. Spoon the lemon curd into the pastry case, then top with the meringue. Return to the oven for 20 minutes, or until the meringue is golden.

Cool to room temperature before serving (or the curd will be too runny).

Serves 18
–
Prep 20 mins, plus chilling
–
Bake 45 mins

PUMPKIN PIE

Canned pumpkin purée makes this recipe a doddle. The filling comes together with a speedy twirl of the balloon whisk and a quick bake to just set the custardy middle. Definitely American Thanksgiving vibes.

For the shortcrust pastry (or use a 500g/1lb 2oz ready-made block)
360g (12½oz) plain (all-purpose) flour, plus extra for dusting
180g (6¼oz) cold unsalted butter, diced into rough 1cm (½in) cubes, plus extra for greasing
4–5 tablespoons ice-cold water

For the filling
260g (9¼oz) caster (superfine) sugar
2 tsp ground cinnamon
1 tsp ground ginger
½ tsp ground cloves
2 eggs, beaten
2 × 400g (14oz) cans pumpkin purée
410g (14½fl oz) can evaporated milk

whipped cream, to serve (optional)

Make the shortcrust pastry dough following the instructions on page 89. Form the dough into a disc, then wrap in cling film (plastic wrap). Refrigerate for 30 minutes.

Preheat the oven to 180°C fan/200°C/400°F/Gas mark 6 and place a large baking sheet inside to preheat. Grease the base and sides of a 20 × 30cm (8 × 12in) baking tray.

When the pastry has chilled, roll it out on a lightly floured surface to form a rectangle measuring about 26 × 36cm (10 × 14in). Gently ease the pastry into the prepared tray. Scrunch up a rectangle of baking parchment to soften it, then lay it over the pastry and fill with baking beads. Place the baking tray on the preheated baking sheet and blind-bake for 15 minutes, then remove the beads and parchment and bake the pastry case for another 10 minutes.

Combine the sugar, spices, eggs, pumpkin purée and evaporated milk in a large bowl and whisk with a balloon whisk until completely combined.

Remove the baked pastry case from the oven and reduce the oven temperature to 160°C fan/180°C/350°F/Gas mark 4. Spoon the pumpkin filling into the pie case and bake for 45–50 minutes, or until there's only the slightest wobble in the centre of the filling.

Serve warm, with whipped cream, if you like.

Serves 20
–
Prep 20 mins, plus chilling
–
Bake 75 mins

FRIDGE
CAKES

When is a traybake not a traybake? When you leave
it to do its thing in the fridge – because sometimes
you don't want to turn the oven on but desperately
need a rocky road. Lots of recipes in this chapter
will lend themselves to baking with little ones, and
they'll definitely be wanting to lick the bowl.

ROCKY ROAD

I think of this as one of the original fridge cakes/ no-bake traybakes. The butter and golden syrup stop the chocolate from setting too hard. The biscuits are a must but the other ingredients are pretty interchangeable – any combination of nuts and dried fruit will do the job.

250g (9oz) salted butter, plus extra for greasing
600g (1lb 5oz) dark chocolate, broken into pieces
6 tbsp golden syrup
400g (14oz) digestive biscuits
125g (4½oz) mini marshmallows
100g (3½oz) toasted hazelnuts, roughly chopped
1 tbsp icing (confectioners') sugar (optional)

Grease and line the base and sides of a 20 × 30cm (8 × 12in) baking tray.

Combine the butter, chocolate and golden syrup in a heatproof bowl set over a pan of barely simmering water. Stir until it has all melted together and is smooth (if you prefer, you can do this in short bursts in the microwave, stirring between each one).

Meanwhile, put the digestive biscuits into a large bowl and use the end of a rolling pin to break into pieces, varying in size so that you have some pieces that are coin-sized and others that are smaller and more crumb-like.

Set aside a third of the melted chocolate mixture (about 330g/11oz), then pour the rest over the biscuits and stir to combine completely. Add the marshmallows and hazelnuts and continue to stir. Transfer this mixture into the prepared tray, spreading it out as flat as possible with the back of the spoon. Spread the reserved chocolate mixture over the top in a thin layer. Refrigerate for at least 3 hours.

Dust with icing sugar (if you like), then use a sharp knife to slice into 24 squares or 18 bars.

Serves 18–24
—
Prep 15 mins, plus chilling

Fridge Cakes

SALTED CARAMEL AND ALMOND CHEESECAKE

The crushed amaretti dotted in the digestive base make this almondy from the bottom up. With a portion of the salted caramel running through the cream cheese filling, and the rest drizzled on top, it's so simple but so decadent.

For the base

200g (7oz) unsalted butter, melted, plus extra for greasing
200g (7oz) digestive biscuits
300g (10½oz) amaretti biscuits

For the filling

400ml (14fl oz) double (heavy) cream
560g (1lb 4oz) full-fat cream cheese
200g (7oz) caster (superfine) sugar
½ tsp almond extract
260g (9¼oz) jarred salted caramel

Grease and line the base and sides of a 20 × 30cm (8 × 12in) baking tray.

To make the base, place the biscuits into a sealable plastic food bag and bash with a rolling pin until finely crushed. (Alternatively, blitz the digestive biscuits in a food processor to form a crumb.) Add the amaretti biscuits and continue to bash or pulse until they are broken down, but don't overmix or they will start to become greasy. Transfer to a bowl and stir in the melted butter, then transfer the mixture to the prepared tray, pushing it down with the back of a spoon to create a nice compact base. Refrigerate while you make the filling.

In a mixing bowl, whisk the cream to soft peaks using a handheld mixer. In a separate mixing bowl, combine the cream cheese, sugar, almond extract and half of the salted caramel, and mix well with the handheld mixer. Fold through the cream, then smooth the mixture on to the biscuit base.

Gently melt the remaining salted caramel in a saucepan over a low heat, then spoon it on to the cream cheese base. Drag a skewer through the caramel to make a swirly pattern, then refrigerate for at least 3 hours before slicing and serving.

Serves 20–24
–
Prep 20 mins, plus chilling

TRIPLE CHOCOLATE CHEESECAKE

With an Oreo biscuit base, milk chocolate middle and white chocolate ganache topping, this slices very impressively – plus, an unbaked cheesecake is such an easy win. As foolproof as you can get!

For the base
180g (6¼oz) salted butter, melted, plus extra for greasing
4 × 154g (5oz) packets of Oreos

For the filling
200g (7oz) dark chocolate, broken into pieces
100g (3½oz) milk chocolate, broken into pieces
325ml (11fl oz) double (heavy) cream
475g (1lb 1oz) full-fat cream cheese
200g (7oz) caster (superfine) sugar
2 tbsp cocoa powder

For the ganache
190ml (6½ fl oz) double (heavy) cream
400g (14oz) white chocolate, chopped into 1cm (½in) pieces, plus extra, grated or shaved into curls, to serve

Grease and line the base and sides of a 20 × 30cm (8 × 12in) baking tray.

To make the base, place the Oreos in a sealable plastic food bag and bash with a rolling pin to form soft crumbs. (Alternatively, whizz the Oreos in a food processor.) Stir in the butter. Spoon the mixture into the prepared tray, pushing it down with the back of a spoon until nicely compact and flattened. Chill for 1 hour.

To make the filling, melt the dark and milk chocolate in a heatproof bowl set over a pan of barely simmering water (if you prefer, you can do this in short bursts in the microwave, stirring between each one). Set aside to cool for 5 minutes.

Put the cream into a large mixing bowl or the bowl of a stand mixer. Whisk until soft peaks form – if you don't have a stand mixer, an electric whisk will make this much easier. In a separate mixing bowl, add the cream cheese and sugar, then sift in the cocoa and stir to combine, then whisk, either by hand or with the electric whisk, until just combined. Stir in the cooled melted chocolate, then gently fold through the whipped cream. Spoon the mixture on to the Oreo base and smooth down so you have a flat surface. Chill while you make the ganache.

Bring the double cream to a gentle simmer in a small saucepan. Put the chopped white chocolate into a heatproof bowl. When the cream starts to steam, pour it over the chocolate and leave to stand for 1 minute, then stir.

Spoon this topping over the chocolate cheesecake filling and carefully smooth out. Refrigerate for a few hours or overnight, then top with the chocolate curls just before slicing and serving.

Serves 24
—
Prep 20 mins, plus chilling

Fridge Cakes

BISCOFF ROCKY ROAD

I truly think Biscoff is one of the best things since sliced bread. I used to aspire to eat a whole jar in one sitting, but now I've found better things to do with it. Combined with white chocolate, it's truly magical – and this is a really worthwhile riff (read: upgrade (!)) on traditional rocky road. It also lasts up to a week stored in an airtight container in the fridge.

75g (2½oz) salted butter, plus extra for greasing
500g (1lb 2oz) white chocolate, broken into pieces
400g (14oz) speculoos biscuits such as Biscoff, broken into pieces
600g (1lb 5oz) smooth biscuit spread, such as Biscoff, melted
100g (3½oz) dried cherries, roughly chopped
125g (4½oz) mini marshmallows

Grease and line the base and sides of a 20 × 30cm (8 × 12in) baking tray.

Melt the white chocolate and butter in a heatproof bowl set over a pan of barely simmering water. Stir until it has all melted together and is smooth (if you prefer, you can do this in short bursts in the microwave, stirring between each one).

Meanwhile, put the Biscoff biscuits into a large bowl and use the end of a rolling pin to break into pieces, varying in size so that you have some pieces that are coin-sized and others that are smaller and more crumb-like.

Stir 150g (5½oz) of the melted Biscoff spread into the white chocolate mixture, then stir again to combine. Pour this mixture over the crushed biscuits and stir to combine completely. Add the dried cherries and marshmallows and stir again. Transfer this mixture to the prepared tray, spreading it out with the back of a spoon. Spread the remaining melted Biscoff spread over the top in a thin layer. Refrigerate for at least 3 hours before slicing and serving.

Serves 24
–
Prep 15 mins, plus chilling

Fridge Cakes

CARAMEL CORNFLAKE SQUARES

These sticky bites are truly dangerous. There's the crunchy cornflake middle, then the more gooey base, all topped with a thick, marbled chocolate layer. The kind of treat you'll want just another sliver of... then another...

160g (5¾oz) salted butter, plus extra
    for greasing
300g (10½oz) soft light brown sugar
200g (7oz) golden syrup
4 tbsp double (heavy) cream
280g (10oz) cornflakes
pinch of salt

For the topping
250g (9oz) dark chocolate, broken
    into pieces
250g (9oz) blonde or white chocolate,
    broken into pieces

Grease and line the base and sides of a 20 × 30cm (8 × 12in) baking tray.

Combine the sugar and golden syrup in a medium saucepan over a low heat. Warm through until the golden syrup becomes more liquid and the sugar starts to dissolve. Add the butter and stir with a wooden spoon to melt, then stir in the cream. Continue to mix until the sugar and butter are melted and combined. Bring to a simmer and allow to bubble for 30 seconds, then remove from the heat and add the cornflakes, along with a pinch of salt. Stir to coat the cornflakes in the caramel sauce.

Spoon the mixture into the prepared tray, pressing down with the back of the spoon to make it nice and compact. Set aside.

To prepare the topping, separately melt the dark and blonde or white chocolate, either in different heatproof bowls set over pans of barely simmering water, or in short bursts in the microwave, stirring between each one.

Dollop alternate spoonfuls of the melted chocolates on top of the cornflake mixture, then use a skewer to marble together. Refrigerate for at least three hours before serving.

Serves 16
—
**Prep 15 mins,
plus chilling**

TRAIL MIX PUFFED RICE SQUARES

Of course, these pay homage to the '90s staple, the Kelloggs Rice Krispie square. With just four ingredients, they're really simple to pull together, and the trail mix filling can be a combination of whatever fruit and nut remnants you have in your cupboards.

75g (2½oz) salted butter, plus extra
for greasing
450g (1lb) marshmallows (mini
or regular)
250g (9oz) puffed rice cereal
300g (10½oz) trail mix (including
chocolate peanuts, if possible)

Grease and line the base and sides of a 20 × 30cm (8 × 12in) baking tray.

Combine the butter and marshmallows in a large saucepan over a low heat and stir until the marshmallows and butter have melted together. Remove from the heat then quickly and carefully stir through the puffed rice cereal and the trail mix. Spoon into the prepared tray and push down with the back of the spoon. Use damp hands to carefully compress the mixture.

Allow to cool before slicing to serve.

Serves 24
–
Prep 15 mins

MINT CHOCOLATE TART

This is a pretty easy dessert to make, and would almost double up as a post-dinner (After Eight?) petit four. The ganache melds the mint chocolates to the biscuit base, and makes for a shiny and smooth finish on top.

100g (3½oz) salted butter, melted, plus extra for greasing
300g (10½oz) bourbon biscuits, crushed
350g (12oz) mint thins (I use After Eights)

For the ganache
110g (3¾oz) salted butter
300g (10½oz) dark chocolate, broken into pieces
2 tbsp golden syrup
200ml (7fl oz) double (heavy) cream

Grease and line the base and sides of a 20 × 30cm (8 × 12in) baking tray.

In a large bowl, combine the crushed bourbon biscuits and melted butter, then spoon the mixture into the base of the prepared tray, pushing it down with the back of the spoon so that it forms a smooth and compact base. Refrigerate for 10 minutes.

Meanwhile, prepare the ganache. Melt the butter, chocolate and golden syrup in a heatproof bowl set over a pan of barely simmering water, stirring until smooth (if you prefer, you can do this in short bursts in the microwave, stirring between each one).

Once melted, take off the heat and add the cream, mixing until smooth. Pour a thin layer of the ganache over the biscuit base, then top with the mint thins, trying to form a nice, smooth layer. Trim some of the mint thins if you need to so you don't have any gaps. Top with the remaining ganache and smooth the top using the back of a spoon or an off-set palette knife. Refrigerate until firm before serving.

Serves 24
–
Prep 20 mins, plus chilling

Fridge Cakes

FLAPJACKS, BARS AND BUNS

This is a chapter of 'others' — a mixed bag of delicious extras that will flex the remnants of your baking muscles. They'll cover breakfast bready bakes to after-school school/post-gym snacks. My favourite might have to be the Peanut Butter Caramel Slice on page 128 — I just can't get enough of it.

CRANBERRY AND CHOCOLATE FLAPJACKS

I grew up with my mum making big trays of flapjacks (and the slightly wishful thinking that they were healthy because they contained oats...). Taking just ten minutes to pull together, they really are a store-cupboard salvation, with the cranberries and dark chocolate chips being offset by the sweetness of the golden syrup mixture.

300g (10½oz) unsalted butter, plus extra for greasing
100g (3½oz) light soft brown sugar
130g (4½oz) golden syrup
450g (1lb) porridge oats
75g (2½oz) desiccated (dried shredded) coconut
150g (5½oz) dried cranberries
200g (7oz) dark chocolate, chopped into small chips, plus 75g (2½oz) to top

Preheat the oven to 170°C fan/190°C/375°F/Gas mark 5. Grease and line the base and sides of a 20 × 30cm (8 × 12in) baking tray.

Combine the butter, sugar and golden syrup in a large saucepan over a low heat and warm through until the butter has melted and the sugar has dissolved. Remove from the heat.

Combine the oats, coconut and dried cranberries in a large bowl and pour the butter mixture over the top. Stir to combine, then leave to rest for 10 minutes.

Now stir through the 200g (7oz) chocolate chips and transfer to the prepared tin. Bake for 25 minutes.

Remove from the oven and slice into 16 bars, then leave to cool, leaving them in the tin.

Once cool, melt the remaining 75g (2½oz) dark chocolate in a heatproof bowl set over a pan of barely simmering water, or in short bursts in the microwave, stirring between each burst. Drizzle over the flapjacks, then transfer to the refrigerator to chill until the chocolate is hardened. Slice again to serve.

Serves 16
—
Prep 15 mins
—
Bake 25 mins

Flapjacks, Bars and Buns

PECAN AND GINGER FLAPJACKS

This batch of flapjacks have a deliciously sweet and buttery undertone of spice. The pecans give that butteriness, while the ginger biscuits almost completely dissolve into the mix, giving pops of caramelized ginger. They're a great, cozy winter treat and will keep for a week in an airtight container.

300g (10½oz) unsalted butter, plus extra for greasing
150g (5½oz) pecans
80g (3oz) light soft brown sugar
130g (4½oz) golden syrup
125g (4½oz) smooth biscuit spread, such as Biscoff
450g (1lb) porridge oats
150g (5½oz) ginger biscuits, broken into small pieces

Preheat the oven to 170°C fan/190°C/375°F/Gas mark 5. Grease and line the base and sides of a 20 × 30cm (8 × 12in) baking tray, and line a separate baking sheet with baking parchment.

Spread out the pecans on the lined baking sheet and bake for 8–10 minutes until smelling toasty. Let cool, then roughly chop. Leave the oven on.

Combine the butter, sugar and golden syrup in a large saucepan over a medium heat and stir until melted together. Stir through the Biscoff spread, followed by the oats, ginger biscuits and pecan pieces. Spoon the mixture into the prepared tray, then press down with the back of a spoon to make it nicely compacted. Bake for 20–25 minutes, or until golden on top.

Slice into 16 bars while still warm, then allow to cool completely before slicing again to serve.

Serves 16
–
Prep 15 mins
–
Bake 35 mins

CINNAMON BUNS

I had to include cinnamon buns because every time I make them, I think 'I should make these more often' (then proceed not to). They're much less intimidating than you might think, and make such an impressive batch bake. A dough hook makes a slightly wetter (and therefore softer) dough a lot more workable, but this is perfectly achievable by hand. They are perfection when enjoyed straight from the oven.

180ml (6fl oz) whole milk
100g (3½oz) unsalted butter, cubed, plus extra for greasing
500g (1lb 2oz) strong white bread flour, plus extra for dusting
7g (¼oz) sachet (packet) instant yeast
1½ tsp ground cinnamon
75g (2½oz) caster (superfine) sugar
2 eggs, beaten

For the filling
180g (6¼oz) soft light brown sugar
2½ tbsp ground cinnamon
150g (5½oz) salted butter, at room temperature

For the icing
75g (2½oz) icing (confectioners') sugar

Heat the milk in a small saucepan over a low heat until gently steaming. Remove from the heat, then add the butter and allow it to melt.

Combine the flour, yeast, cinnamon and sugar in a large bowl, or in the bowl of a stand mixer fitted with a dough hook. Add the eggs and combine briefly, either with a spatula or with the dough hook, then add the milk and butter mixture. Knead the dough on a lightly floured surface for around 10 minutes, or until silky and elastic, if working by hand. Alternatively, knead with the dough hook for 5–7 minutes. Set aside in a lightly greased bowl covered with cling film (plastic wrap) or a clean dish towel and leave to prove for 1–1½ hours, or until doubled in size.

Grease and line the base and sides of a 20 × 30cm (8 × 12in) baking tray.

To make the filling, combine the light brown sugar, cinnamon and butter in a bowl to form a paste.

Once the dough has finished proving, push it back to get rid of any air bubbles, then roll it out on a floured surface to form a rectangle measuring 30 × 40cm (12 × 16in). Spread the cinnamon butter all over the rectangle, right to the edges. With the dough in a landscape orientation, tightly roll it up, pushing it away from you. Use a sharp knife to slice the roll into 12 pieces. Place these in the prepared tray and cover with cling film or a clean dish towel. Prove for another 20–30 minutes, or until the buns have expanded and are almost touching one another.

Meanwhile, preheat the oven to 180°C fan/200°C/400°F/Gas mark 6. Bake the buns for 25–30 minutes, or until golden brown. Enjoy warm, or allow to cool to room temperature. When you're ready to eat, make the icing by sifting the icing sugar into a bowl, then combine with 1 tablespoon of wate. Drizzle over the buns to serve.

Makes 12
–
Prep 40 mins, plus proving
–
Bake 30 mins

COFFEE AND CARDAMOM BUNS

If you needed another excuse to make the house smell delicious, enter the coffee and cardamom bun. The subtle spice goes so well with the coffee tones, giving rich and slightly bitter vibes simultaneously. Once the buns are rolled and sliced, try doing the second prove overnight in the fridge, so you can have deliciously fresh baked buns for breakfast.

seeds from 10 cardamom pods
75g (2½oz) caster (superfine) sugar
180ml (6fl oz) whole milk
1 tbsp instant coffee
100g (3½oz) unsalted butter, cubed,
　　plus extra for greasing
500g (1lb 2oz) strong white bread flour,
　　plus extra for dusting
7g (¼oz) sachet (packet) instant yeast
2 eggs, beaten

For the filling
180g (6¼oz) soft light brown sugar
150g (5½oz) salted butter, at room
　　temperature
1 tbsp instant coffee
seeds from 10 cardamom pods

For the icing
75g (2½oz) icing (confectioners') sugar
1 tbsp instant coffee

Using a pestle and mortar, grind the cardamom seeds to a powder with a pinch of the caster (superfine) sugar. Combine the milk, coffee and ground cardamom in a medium saucepan over a low heat until gently steaming. Remove from the heat, then add the butter and allow it to melt.

Combine the flour, yeast and remaining sugar in a large mixing bowl, or in the bowl of a stand mixer fitted with a dough hook. Add the eggs and combine briefly, either with a spatula or with the dough hook, then add the milk and butter mixture. Knead the dough on a lightly floured surface for around 10 minutes, or until silky and elastic, if working by hand. Alternatively, knead with the dough hook for 5–7 minutes. Set aside in a lightly greased bowl covered with cling film (plastic wrap) or a clean dish towel and leave to prove for 1–1½ hours, or until doubled in size.

Grease and line the base and sides of a 20 × 30cm (8 × 12in) baking tray.

To prepare the filling, use a pestle and mortar to grind the cardamom seeds and coffee to a powder. Transfer to a bowl and add the light brown sugar and butter. Mix to form a paste.

Once the dough has finished proving, push it back to get rid of any air bubbles, then roll it out on a floured surface to form a rectangle measuring 30 × 40cm (12 × 16in). Spread the coffee and cardamom butter all over the rectangle, right to the edges. With the dough in a landscape orientation, tightly roll it up, pushing it away from you. Use a sharp knife to slice the roll into 12 pieces. Place these in the prepared tray and cover with cling film or a clean dish towel. Prove for another 20–30 minutes, or until the buns have expanded and are almost touching one another.

Meanwhile, preheat the oven to 180°C fan/200°C/400°F/Gas mark 6. Bake the buns for 25–30 minutes until golden brown.

To make the icing, dissolve the instant coffee in 1 tablespoon boiling water in a bowl, then sift in the icing sugar and mix to combine. Drizzle this over the buns, and serve warm or cold.

Makes 12
–
Prep 30 mins,
plus proving
–
Bake 30 mins

PEANUT BUTTER CARAMEL SLICE

Think millionaire's shortbread with a peanut butter twist – essentially a shortbread biscuit base with peanut caramel and a sumptuous, marbled chocolate top. This is criminally easy to eat and the perfect fix with a cup of tea. It will last up to a week in an airtight container in the fridge.

210g (7½oz) cold unsalted butter, diced into rough 1cm (½in) cubes, plus extra for greasing
250g (9oz) plain (all-purpose) flour
125g (4½oz) caster (superfine) sugar
1 tsp vanilla bean paste

For the caramel
100g (3½oz) unsalted butter
397g (14oz) can condensed milk
40g (1½oz) golden syrup
30g (1oz) soft light brown sugar
150g (5½oz) smooth peanut butter
flaky sea salt

For the topping
300g (10½oz) dark chocolate, broken into pieces
40g (1½oz) unsalted butter
50g (2oz) smooth peanut butter

Preheat the oven to 160°C fan/180°C/350°F/Gas mark 4. Grease and line the base and sides of a 20 × 30cm (8 × 12in) baking tray.

In a large bowl, rub the flour and butter together with your fingertips until sandy. (Alternatively, combine the flour and butter in a food processor and pulse until sandy.) Add the sugar and vanilla and pulse again. Tip into the prepared tray and push down with the back of a spoon until nicely compacted. Bake for 20 minutes, or until lightly golden.

Meanwhile, to make the caramel, combine the butter, condensed milk, golden syrup and sugar in a saucepan with a large pinch of flaky sea salt. Heat over a low heat, stirring gently until the sugar and butter melt together. Increase the heat and cook for 5½ minutes, stirring constantly. Remove from the heat and stir through the 150g (5oz) peanut butter until combined.

Remove the baked biscuit base from the oven. Smooth the caramel on to the base and allow to cool and set completely.

For the topping, melt the dark chocolate with the butter in a heatproof bowl set over a pan of barely simmering water (if you prefer, do this in short bursts in the microwave, stirring between each one). Drizzle the melted chocolate over the set caramel to make a flat surface. In a saucepan, lightly warm the peanut butter through to loosen it slightly, then spoon the peanut butter over the top of the chocolate in lines. Drag a skewer sideways across the lines to make a chevron effect. Sprinkle with a little extra flaky sea salt. Slice into 24 bars.

Serves 24
–
Prep 20 mins
–
Bake 20 mins

DATE AND WALNUT BARS

This is a really straightforward recipe and lands you with some delicious energy bars. The beauty of Medjool dates is their natural sweetness and fudginess, so you end up with a fairly guilt-free pick-me-up, packed full of flavour.

500g (1lb 2oz) Medjool dates, pitted
100g (3½oz) coconut oil, melted, plus extra for greasing
350g (12oz) walnuts, roughly chopped
150g (5½oz) smooth peanut butter
150g (5½oz) mixed seeds

Put the dates in a bowl and pour over enough boiling water to cover. Leave to soak for 20 minutes.

Grease and line the base and sides of a 20 × 30cm (8 × 12in) baking tray. Preheat the oven to 150°C fan/170°C/340°F/ Gas mark 3½.

Drain the soaked dates and tip them into a food processor, along with 200g (7oz) of the walnuts. Blitz to form a purée, then add the peanut butter and coconut oil and mix to combine. Transfer to a bowl and mix through the remaining walnuts and the seeds, then spoon the mixture into the prepared tray, pushing it down with the back of the spoon.

Bake for 20 minutes, or until the top is longer tacky. Cool, then slice into bars to serve.

Serves 24
–
Prep 10 mins
–
Bake 20 mins

FIG BARS

With these containing dried figs, I can almost mentally claim them as healthy. Unsubstantiated health claims aside, these are a hybrid of cake and biscuit, filled with a smooth but crunchy figgy filling, and are a great bar for taking on picnics or walks!

For the filling
750g (1lb 10oz) dried figs,
    roughly chopped
120g (4¼oz) caster (superfine) sugar

For the bars
320g (11¼oz) unsalted butter, plus extra
    for greasing
240g (8½oz) caster (superfine) sugar
2 eggs, beaten
460g (1lb ½oz) plain (all-purpose) flour
80g (3oz) porridge oats
¾ tsp baking powder

Begin by making the filling. Combine the figs and sugar with 150ml (5fl oz) water in a medium saucepan. Place over a low–medium heat for 7–10 minutes, or until the figs are starting to break down and the liquid is thick and glossy. Allow to cool. Add an extra 2 tablespoons of water to the pan, then use a stick blender to partly purée the mixture, so you still have some fig pieces.

Preheat the oven to 160°C fan/180°C/350°F/Gas mark 4. Grease and line the base and sides of a 20 × 30cm (8 × 12in) baking tray.

To make the batter, combine the butter and sugar in a large mixing bowl, or the bowl of a stand mixer, and whisk until creamy. Beat in the eggs, then stir through the flour, oats and baking powder. Smooth half the mixture over the base of the prepared tray, then top with the fig mixture. Top with the remaining batter and smooth it over the figs. Bake for 40 minutes.

Make markings into the sponge while still warm (to make it easier to cut later). Cool before slicing and serving.

Serves 18
–
Prep 30 mins
–
Bake 40 mins

APRICOT CRUMBLE SLICE

I can confess to being most besotted with this recipe. The combination of apricot conserve with the chopped dried apricots gives a sticky but soft topping to the shortbready base. And, as I mentioned in the recipe on page 91, crumble makes everything better. I invite you to also become obsessed.

320g (11¼oz) cold unsalted butter, diced into rough 1cm (½in) cubes, plus extra for greasing
375g (13oz) plain (all-purpose) flour
180g (6¼oz) caster (superfine) sugar
1 tsp vanilla bean paste
200g (7oz) dried apricots, diced
370g (13oz) apricot conserve
80g (2¾oz) porridge oats
100g (3½oz) light soft brown sugar

vanilla custard, to serve

Preheat the oven to 160°C fan/180°C/350°F/Gas mark 4. Grease and line the base and sides of a 20 × 30cm (8 × 12in) baking tray.

Rub the butter into the flour using your fingertips until a sandy mixture forms. (Alternatively, pulse the flour and butter in a food processor.) Add the sugar and vanilla and mix or pulse again to combine. Remove a third of the mixture (about 280g/10oz) and set aside in a bowl in the refrigerator, then tip the rest into the prepared tray and push it down with the back of a spoon to form a compact base. Bake for 20 minutes, or until lightly golden.

In a bowl, combine the diced apricots with the apricot conserve, then spread over the baked shortbread base.

In a separate bowl, combine the remaining shortbread dough (from the refrigerator) with the oats and brown sugar, breaking up any big clumps of mixture. Scatter this over the apricot filling and bake for another 30 minutes. Cool slightly, then slice and serve at room temperature with custard.

Serves 18–24
–
Prep 15 mins
–
Bake 50 mins

Flapjacks, Bars and Buns

PLUM JAM LAMINGTONS

There are lots of conflicting stories about the origin of the lamington (many involving Queensland, Australia, and one that claims that a tray of cakes were dropped in gravy, then rolled in desiccated coconut to hide the misdemeanour). Whatever the truth may be, they do involve some hands-on time to get to the end result, but the reward is delicious. I love plum jam with chocolate, but exchange it for whatever you have in your pantry.

200g (7oz) salted butter, at room
    temperature, plus extra for greasing
200g (7oz) golden caster
    (superfine) sugar
3 eggs, beaten
220g (8oz) self-raising flour
¼ tsp fine salt
75ml (5 tablespoons) whole milk
100–150g (3½–5½oz) plum jam

For the icing
450g (1lb) icing (confectioners') sugar
50g (2oz) cocoa powder
50g (2oz) salted butter, at room
    temperature, chopped
110ml (3¾fl oz) boiling water

To finish
250g (9oz) desiccated (dried shredded)
    coconut

Preheat the oven to 160°C fan/180°C/350°F/Gas mark 4. Grease and line the base and sides of a 20 × 30cm (8 × 12in) baking tray.

Combine the butter and sugar in a large mixing bowl, or the bowl of a stand mixer, and whisk until pale and fluffy. Slowly add the eggs, whisking until combined, then sift in the flour. Fold through, along with the salt and milk. Spoon the mixture into the prepared tray and smooth the top. Bake for 30 minutes, then allow to cool completely in the tray.

Once cool, remove from the baking tray and cut the sponge in half through the middle to create two layers. Spread the cut-side of the bottom half with the plum jam, then top with the top half of cake. Refrigerate for 20 minutes to firm up, then cut into 20 rectangles.

To make the icing, sift the icing sugar and cocoa into a bowl. Place the butter in a separate bowl and pour the boiling water over the top. Stir to melt. Add this mixture to the icing sugar and cocoa, and stir to make a loose icing.

Tip half the desiccated coconut into a bowl and prepare a wire rack. Using two skewers, lift one of the sandwiched cakes and carefully dip it into the icing, using a spoon to ensure it's completely covered, and allowing the excess to drip off. Transfer to the bowl of coconut and carefully remove the skewers. Use two forks to gently toss the cake in the coconut. Transfer to the wire rack and repeat with the remaining cakes, icing and coconut, replenishing the coconut bowl as needed (so it doesn't all get coated in icing). Chill to harden before serving.

Serves 20
–
**Prep 20 mins,
plus chilling**
–
Bake 30 mins

NO-BAKE FUDGE SQUARES

These squares are pure energy gold – the lovechild of fudge and flapjacks, they're dense but soft and intensely sweet. The bitter chocolate topping is the perfect counter to the biscuity base. It could be the perfect excuse to use up those last few digestive biscuits...

300g (10½oz) salted butter, plus extra for greasing
325g (11½oz) digestive biscuits
150g (5½oz) porridge oats
100g (3½oz) golden syrup
397g (14oz) can condensed milk
215g (7½oz) soft light brown sugar
large pinch of flaky sea salt
400g (14oz) dark chocolate, broken into pieces

Grease and line the base and sides of a 20 × 30cm (8 × 12in) baking tray.

Combine the digestive biscuits and oats in a food processor and pulse until the digestives are crumbs and the oats have broken down.

Combine the golden syrup, butter, condensed milk, light brown sugar and salt in a medium saucepan over a medium heat. Stir for about 5 minutes to melt together, then stir through the crumbled digestives and oats.

Spoon the mixture into the prepared baking tray and smooth the top, then leave to cool to room temperature.

Melt the chocolate in a heatproof bowl set over a pan of barely simmering water (if you prefer, do this in short bursts in the microwave, stirring between each one). Smooth the melted chocolate over the no-bake bake. Chill to firm up, then slice and serve.

Serves 20
–
Prep 15 mins

INDEX

ACKNOWLEDGEMENTS

A big thanks to my mum and Auntie Diane for founding and nourishing my great love of baking! I grew up with a lot of recipes written in cup measures, scrawled into little notebooks, stained with butter and the memories of past bakes. Having access to Diane's American recipes and the gigantic bags of chocolate chips that only seemed to exist in the USA in the '90s meant that I knew what a really good chocolate chip cookie was from a very young age – and the bar was set high for life. Every time I eat carrot cake, I think of you, and always will. Mum's homemade birthday cakes were always the kindest and most beautiful creations. You two ladies showed me that baking IS love!

To my gorgeous man, Justin – who claims to not have a sweet tooth. Thank you for 'forcing' yourself to try every bake (at least once), and for encouraging me to take on this project when we were already juggling 17 exciting balls. You always accept my tired tears with such patience and are my perfect tonic. And to my gorgeous boy, Teddy – your approval of my bakes is the highest compliment. You'll always be Chef One to my Chef Two. Dad – thanks for letting me take over your kitchen for the second half of this book (and a lot of my adult life). Your tolerance for my mess is remarkable.

To every author whose baking book I've worked on – your wealth of knowledge and attention to detail has made me the baker I am today! In the 12 years of working on photo shoots, I never thought I would have the chance to collate 60 of my own baking recipes, so this has been an absolute dream. Sofie Shearman – thank you for the magical opportunity and for bending your schedule to fit me in! Your kind encouragement has boosted my confidence and made me so proud of what we have achieved together. Katy Everett – the design is perfect. Thanks for nailing it.

Rita Platts – I couldn't be happier with the photography. You put together sets with the most effortless elegance, and such a cool touch. I want to live in our book!!! The memories of our shoot days will be as treasured as the photos you took. Thank you, Max Robinson, for creating the world inside these pages with your stunning propping. I was so glad we could work together on this. Our careers have progressed alongside each other's and I'm so overjoyed to see what we're both achieving.

To my tireless assistants, Jess, Lucy and Mimi, thanks for lining tins over and over again, washing up buttery bowls and lugging crates up and down stairs. Thanks for being turbo bakers in the prep kitchen while I faffed about on set. Jess – I think your praise of my pastry might be the equivalent to Paul Hollywood's golden handshake? I'm very lucky to have had your baking skills, hilarious company and support throughout this whole process. It's been a blast!